OPERATION
CHARISMA

Also by JOHN M. CURTIS, Ph.D.

Dodging The Bullet

DISCOBOLOS

™

WHEN PERFECTION
IS THE ONLY OPTION

OPERATION
CHARISMA

How to
Get Charisma
and Wind Up At the Top

JOHN M. CURTIS, Ph.D.

DISCOBOLOS PRESS
Los Angeles • New York

© Copyright 1999 John M. Curtis and Discobolos Press ®

Published by: Discobolos Press ®   Tel (310) 204-8300 • Fax (310) 440-0015

11777 San Vicente Blvd., Suite 703   157 E. 18th St., Suite 1-C
West Los Angeles, CA 90049   New York, NY 10003

Orders and Logistics: Technical Book Co., Inc.   Tel (800) 233-5150
                                 2036 Westwood Blvd.   Fax (310) 470-9810
                                 Los Angeles, CA 90025

First Edition: September 1999

Printed in the United States of America

Paperback 10 9 8 7 6 5 4 3 2 1

Library of Congress Catalog Card Number: 99-93578

ISBN: 0-9670327-0-9

Curtis, John M.
    Operation Charisma: *How to Get Charisma and Wind Up at the Top*
    1. Self-help. 2. Business. 3. Psychology. 4. Management. 5. Communications.
    6. Public Relations.

Manuscript Reviewers: Dr. Valerie Susman, Dr. Mimi Curtis & Dr. Daniela Vignale
Manuscript Editor & Proofreader: Ms. Marie Claire Erde
Cover Design: DGD Phototypesetting
Typesetting: DGD Phototypesetting

For

G.T.K.

Who Set The Benchmark

CONTENTS

ACKNOWLEDGMENTS

While much of what's contained in OPERATION CHARISMA is based on 20 years of my research and consulting practice, many unnamed voices deserve recognition. Creative projects are rarely inspired or produced in a vacuum. Among the many influences--including past mentors, students, friends and, yes, clients--the linkages can never be forgotten or disowned, despite the faded contact. At the same time, reading through the work, there's little doubt that I've borrowed from many different sources. On that note, you've all shaped OPERATION CHARISMA.

Unfurling the mystery of charisma was no small undertaking. Asking charismatic people to share their secrets usually draws blanks: Not--in my view--from their unwillingness to divulge their secrets, but truly from their inability to recognize and communicate those subtle essences [*high-level intangibles*], which make them successful. OPERATION CHARISMA infiltrates those 'classified' secrets and reveals their magic. Some closer to the source have even suggested that OPERATION CHARISMA shares just as much about the author. On that note, I won't take exception.

The author gratefully acknowledges the many individuals connected with OPERATION CHARISMA:

to my fine research and consulting staff, Dr. Mimi Curtis, Mr. Robert Curtis, Dr. Valerie Susman, Dr. Daniela Vignale, Dr. Preston Oppenheimer and Mr. Marc Hamer, whose stimulating discussions and many suggestions greatly added to the work's substance;

to Dr. Tony Alessandra, Mr. Brian Tracy and Mr. Zig Zigler, whose encouraging words, 'advance praise' and belief in the manuscript, helped inspire the work to fruition;

to my literary agent Ms. Jayne Rockmill, whose enduring faith, unrewarded work and savvy suggestions improved the marketability of the work;

to Geoffrey Berkin, Esq., whose suggestion to 'write a book' can't go unnoticed and whose copyright expertise has been an invaluable resource;

to James Seltzer, Esq., whose professionalism, sagacious predictions and effervescent positive energy helped push the envelope;

to Miguel Drobinsky, M.D., whose wisdom, poetry and unparalleled altruism constitutes a living tribute to the reality of charisma;

to my editorial staff, Dr. Susman, Dr. Curtis and Dr. Vignale whose patience and sleepless nights were spent pouring over the endless revisions and changes;

to my editor and proofreader, Ms. Marie Claire Erde, whose meticulous reviews of the manuscript detected the undetectable and whose editorial precision honed and polished the finished product;

to Mr. Paul Hirdler, Mr. Dennis Farrell and Ms. Pamela Wanzer at Delta Direct Access for their publishing expertise and profesionalism; and finally,

to all the prospective readers, whose desire to succeed knows no limits but whose charismatic skills need some polish, I promise you that I haven't pulled any punches and trust that OPERATION CHARISMA will help light up your path.

FOREWORD

We choose to go to the moon. We choose to go to the moon in this decade and do the other things, not because they are easy, but because they are hard...

John F. Kennedy

Our search for the 'magic bullets' of success leads us beyond strategies and tactics into the uncharted zone of charisma. Sifting through the many unlabeled variables, we stumbled upon some mercurial but verifiable elements which seem to underlie this slippery phenomenon. We refer to these indispensable factors as *high-level intangibles* because they're unmeasurable by most conventional standards but truly responsible for an individual's success. The fact that these special qualities are more stealth-like, less easy to recognize and difficult to teach, doesn't mean they're unworthy of our attention.

Practiced routinely by highly successful people, they represent talents poorly understood but clearly, in the final analysis, responsible for an individual's success. High-level intangibles transcend technical training, expertise or competency--for skill-mastery is only one small part of the success equation. Many well trained and highly competent people find success eluding their grasp. While they've mastered many important details or facts, they've missed the vehicle for putting all the ingredients into a winning formula.

While many people believe that charisma is inborn and untrainable, identifying the high-level intangibles on which it's based now helps pave the way for accelerated learning. By familiarizing yourself with and rehearsing high-level intangibles, anyone with normal intelligence, enough motivation and diligent practice can increase charisma. Although learning new things rarely comes easy, individuals are pleasantly surprised at how quickly these coveted skills are learned and executed. By following the book's logic and vivid illustrations, the path to charisma is more clearly marked.

OPERATION CHARISMA is essentially a how-to book for developing charisma and improving success in business and everyday life. It categorically rejects the idea that charisma is a natural phenomenon which can't be taught. The book is formatted to first present a detailed discussion of a topic and then follow with a dialogue providing a real-life scenario. Readers are treated to the most realistic application of theoretical material possible by carefully following the interaction in the dialogue. Following the dialogue, readers are walked through an analysis of what transpired, relating the repartee back to key ideas and concepts.

By illustrating the book's ideas with real-life dialogues, readers observe directly the actual *words and phrases* exchanged, providing the most concrete way possible--short of role playing--of understanding the material presented. As most coaches or teachers know, there's no one way of learning and probably no magical shortcuts. But most trainers agree that rehearsal and repetition are the path to mastery. While OPERATION CHARISMA can't be everything to everybody, special effort was made to relate to the widest cross section of people. Many different scenarios from various walks of life illustrate the book's concepts.

The book opens with *High-Level Intangibles* [Chapter 1] presenting the essential building blocks on which OPERATION CHARISMA is based. These concepts represent the unifying themes running through the entire book. Teaching high-level intangibles--the verifiable elements of charisma--is a major objective of the book. Offering the philosophical spine of this work, *Narcissism On the Ropes* [Chapter 2] makes the case that you can't effectively apply high-level intangibles unless you abandon self-centered propensities. Discussing the relationship between charisma and relating, *It's All About Relating* [Chapter 3] suggests that charisma can't be maintained without effective relating. Examining the notion of credibility, *Credibility On the Line* [Chapter 4] raises the idea that charisma and credibility are inseparably related. Finally, the book ends with *Charisma Inside Out* [Chapter 5] exploring the other side of the charisma equation together with practical applications.

Like the force of gravity, charisma exerts a powerful but equally disguised effect on human interaction. Some people question its existence, but those intoxicated by its force and consumed with its influence know intuitively that it's real. While OPERATION CHARISMA dissects and focuses on its unique properties, it has no control over the purposes for which it's eventually used. Readers are alerted to the difference between manipulators and truly charismatic people. Unlike social predators--also known as con artists or sociopaths--charismatic people do their utmost to enhance the lives of others. As most people know, manipulators are clearly out for themselves.

While it's easy to ignore the darker side, unconscious neediness magnifies perceptions of charisma, even where none exists. The more abysmal the neediness, the more distorted and exaggerated the aura of charisma. As you can guess, 'hearing what *you* believe and believing what *you* hear,' has some risky consequences. Individuals mesmerized by the enchanting spell of 'charisma' are duly forewarned.

As we've seen, 'the road to success is always under construction.' And while it's been said that it's better to be lucky than good,' the truth is that it's better to be lucky *and* good. By refining *high-level intangibles* and developing charisma, savvy students of success are one quantum leap closer.

John M. Curtis
Los Angeles
July 18, 1998

Chapter *1*

HIGH-LEVEL INTANGIBLES

In this chapter you'll learn about the many high-level intangibles involved in charisma. • Introduction • Savoir faire, tact and face-saving • Common sense • Diplomacy • Timing • Awareness and insight • Politeness and manners • Energy and motivation • Experience and good judgment • Drive and desire • Charm, class and grace under pressure • Playfulness and humor • Some final thoughts • Points to remember

Introduction

High-level intangibles are verifiable talents not easily seen but clearly responsible for an individual's success. When performing most activities, technical skills can only take you so far before finesse either takes over or deserts you. Having superior grades or the best 'numbers' is also no assurance of success. Without 'common sense' and a host of other intangibles you're facing an uphill battle. When panning for gold, it's not your method but your instincts or intangibles which determine your fate--discipline and hard work can only take you so far.

Staying on the right trail is more than following a well-defined map--it's about allowing your internal compass or *high-level intangibles* to guide you toward your goal. It's the 'third eye' or intuition which serves as a type of gyroscope keeping you on your feet, when gravity or a slippery slope would have you on your wallet! While learning strategies for making *politically correct* responses has its place, OPERATION CHARISMA transcends tactics and cultivates the many high-level intangibles underlying charisma and responsible for success. By developing charisma, manipulation and game-playing eventually become less relevant to orchestrate your agenda.

For those unlucky individuals whose technical skills pass the grade but whose high-level intangibles don't measure up, they sadly wind up losing their way. Forever attributing success to some divine kismet or luck, these same individuals envy those 'lucky' devils whose education, training or skills aren't *Phi Beta Kappa* but whose *high-level intangibles* usually wind up saving their rear-ends and assuring success.

Although many people rely heavily on good training and preparation, they can't ad-lib enough to achieve their goals. Or, if they do reach their goals, it's not long before they fall off the pedestal. It's sometimes said that without the special first-aid of these unique talents--high-level intangibles--life becomes a high-wire act of relying on lady luck to carry you through difficult situations. Charisma, or the adroit application of high-level intangibles, affords the extra margin of safety to get results.

There are many examples of high-level intangibles, including, *savoir faire*, tact and face-saving, diplomacy, energy and motivation, drive and desire, experience and good judgment, common sense, timing, awareness and sensitivity, politeness and good manners, charm, class and grace-under-pressure, playfulness and humor or any other quality not usually part of some organized training program in either school or work. For the lucky ones, they've picked up some of these special abilities while growing up. For others less fortunate, they've spent considerable time suffering, attempting to unlearn bad habits absorbed early in life, forever seeking better role-models.

For the vast majority, they've sweated bullets in the school of hard-knocks, learning important lessons slowly, with considerable pain. As most people know, although ultimately there may be no short cuts, gleaning helpful tips from life--while time-consuming--is by no means impossible. Paying closer attention and developing the subtle elements of charisma can make the difference between success and failure.

Without an appreciation and show of these qualities, life's many rewards can elude your grasp. Learning these special talents is easier said than done. It takes, first, an awareness that these intangibles do, in fact, exist and, second, that they can, in fact, be learned. Although learning new skills is labor-intensive, it's all within reach if there's enough motivation and desire. While life-experience has its place, it's not the only method by which learning occurs. Certainly, the training paradigm in which it's possible to learn from instruction or the shared experiences of others, represents the next best hope for accelerating the learning process.

A senior vice president in the movie industry is known for lecturing his colleagues at development meetings. Always sounding an imperious tone, he's lavish with his opinions and short on his listening skills. At a meeting with his staff to determine the company's next project, he shares his views:

"I'm absolutely convinced that the market is saturated with romantic comedies. Like dessert, the viewing public always has a little more room for another Sci-Fi film. Anybody who thinks that it's the right time for another romantic comedy is off their rocker!"

Responding to his insulting remarks, his development executive takes exception to his contentious opinions and says:

"Bill, we know that you have your opinions. But you have to accept the fact that most of us disagree with you. The staff believes that our romantic comedy project is a total winner."

Now feeling challenged and ganged up on, Bill lashes out:

"I'm putting you all on notice: If this film flops, heads are going to roll! I'm going on record opposing this ridiculous project."

Feeling bullied and offended, another member of the development team speaks up:

"Bill, with all due respect, there's obviously no way that any of us can work with you any more. We're simply not going to take your abuse any longer."

Paying close attention to the flow of the conversation, it's not difficult to see that Bill is bankrupt of diplomatic and tactful ways of communicating with his staff. Instead of inviting dialogue, he's insulting and intimidating. He's created an untenable situation for his staff on whom he's dependent for successful projects. Because of his boorish behavior, he's alienated his staff who no longer want to work with him. By learning to express himself in more tactful ways, he might have been able to persuade a reluctant staff to accept his views. Showing intolerance and expressing himself in unacceptable ways, he's failed to orchestrate his agenda. Pushing people around, bullying and intimidating have no place in the lives of charismatic people.

Savoir Faire, Tact and Face-Saving

Orchestrating your agenda requires the awareness that it's not done in a vacuum without having an effect on others. As long as you don't consider the impact of your words or actions on anyone else, you can expect to be a loser many times over. Charisma involves developing the tact to address the needs of someone else and figuring out how to do or say something in a manner that's comfortable to others.

What's tolerable to you or what you find 'funny,' isn't necessarily what's acceptable to anyone else. Making your best guess of what it's like to be in another person's shoes, is a good initial step in learning tact. In other words, it might be well if you'd ask yourself, "If I do or say such-and-such, what effect will it have?" This awareness is most helpful in trying to diagnose another person's reactions.

Essentially, it's about measuring the condition of a person's ego. Once you get a sense of the degree of security or weakness, you can adjust your tact or strategy to accommodate someone else's needs. Without this step, wasteful amounts of energy and resources can be spent in head-to-head combat resulting in little or nothing gained. In fact, it might be worse in the sense that you've depleted your own resources--and your wallet--for a cause that bears no tangible rewards.

A CEO and chairman of the board, Bill, for a mega-financial institution has been bitter enemies of their main arch-rival for nearly 30 years. For more than 3 decades, they've fought tooth-and-nail for market-share and jockeyed for the bragging rights of "who's the biggest." There's no love lost between the boards and certainly their long-standing chairmen. After fluctuating market conditions, the institution is facing financial woes and is now ripe for acquisition. The chief financial officer [CFO] on the board has been tendered a lucrative buy-out offer by their old competitor. Facing his loyal directors at an emergency board meeting, the chairman responds to the buyout offer:

"Over my dead body would I ever accept an offer to merge our company with Gump's bank. I don't give a hoot how much they've offered! We'll never surrender to his group."

Noting the obvious emotional tone to the chairman's remarks, the CFO, Jim, responds:

"Bill, I totally understand the way you feel. I don't blame you for feeling that way. We all know the long war you've been in for the last 30 years building our company. Believe me, I'd love to do what you want! But what do we say to our shareholders when they ask why we didn't accept their stock offer which was more than $5.00 per share greater than the closest bidder?" Reacting defensively and showing some annoyance, the CEO responds:

"Jim, I don't care what you tell our shareholders . . . I'm not surrendering to the enemy at any price!" Sensing the chairman's recalcitrance, the CFO says:

"Bill, you have every right to feel as you do. But we'd shoot ourselves in the foot, if we took the lesser bid. Please try to reconsider what's best for the company."

After an agonizing debate inside the board, they followed the wishes and will of their CEO and took the offer of the company with the lower bid. The chairman and the board's egos were also so badly bruised that they flat-out refused to take the best offer. Recognizing that egos are powerful things goes a long way in avoiding the types of wasteful confrontations which involve actually sacrificing someone's best interests to save face. Had the board or the CFO given the CEO a face-saving way out, he might have considered negotiating a better deal. Allowing damaged egos to get in the way of sound business decisions occurs more readily than one admits. Battling Titanic-sized egos is a no-win situation and best avoided whenever possible.

When encountering ego problems, it's helpful to (a) recognize what or with whom you're dealing and (b) plan a careful strategy to avoid paying an excessive price for nothing but aggravation. Most troubled egos can be easily placated and massaged along just enough to accomplish your agenda. As a good rule of thumb, play your cards close to the vest. Don't wear your emotions on your sleeve, especially when they involve love or hate relationships. By showing your emotions, you risk antagonizing otherwise cooperative individuals and creating the kind of defensiveness which makes getting your way all the more difficult.

A deranged and tyrannical despot is once again threatening his neighbors and destabilizing world peace. The world community has grown increasingly nervous as he continues developing weapons of mass destruction. Pushing the world to the brink of war, the secretary of state orders another round of gunboat diplomacy. A flotilla of war ships are dispatched to the region. The ultimatum is clear: Conform or face the music. Speaking about the U.S. position to the press, the secretary of state remarks:

"We've re-deployed our carrier task forces back to the region to let the world know that the U.S. means business. Rogue nations will not be tolerated now or ever."

Having an expansive ego and feeling boxed into a corner, the despot responds through his emissary:

"We will *not* negotiate with the American devil. And we will *not* be humiliated. With Allah on our side, we're prepared for the 'Mother' of all battles. We're prepared to die to defend our homeland."

After breaking off discussions with the U.S., the secretary of state decides to pass the diplomacy buck to the secretary-general of the United Nations. Known for his mild mannered style and *savoir faire* he gains access to the despot and tells him:

"You are a great leader with a great country. No one wants war--certainly not the U.N.. We know how persistent the Americans can be. Let's try to placate them by giving them what they think they want. You want your dignity . . . they [the Americans] want inspections. Let's require all inspections to be accompanied by qualified diplomatic personnel. You get what you want--and they get what they *think* they want. Above all, we all avoid a senseless and counterproductive war. How about it? Seem reasonable? Let's do it!"

After moving beyond the battleground of egos, giving the deranged despot a face-saving way out, and declaring that the other side has made all the concessions, the secretary general struck a deal acceptable to both sides. Regardless of who got the better end of the bargain, tact and diplomacy were used to pull it off. Knowing the Titanic size of the despot's ego, the secretary general made a tactical decision to placate him. By stroking him and giving the impression that he negotiated the best deal, he was able to save face and eventually cut a deal. Whatever the venue, as long as it's a battle of proud but fragile egos, there's little room for meaningful negotiation.

Common Sense

Like prospecting for certain precious minerals, 'common sense' is also in short supply. Although it seems easy for some, many individuals misfire when it comes to common sense. By being too myopic and focusing on excessive theoretical or technical minutia, projecting their own idiosyncratic views on the situation, or simply missing essential information, common sense has an uncanny way of deserting people when they need it most. Miscalculations easily occur when neediness blinds one from honing in on essential facts used to make intelligent decisions.

A beleaguered psychotherapist, finding himself financially strapped by the current unforgiving health care system, is praying against all odds to be rescued. Finding less reimbursement for his services and having difficulty meeting his monthly nut, he reads an ad in a trade publication promising to give him training to write prescriptions. Although he knows it's currently unlawful for non-physicians to write prescriptions, he's euphoric about the prospects. He reviews the ad with perhaps inflated enthusiasm:

"Receive specialized training to *eventually* write prescriptions and sign-up for charter membership in the American Association of Prescribing Mental Health Practitioners. The home-study training course is offered for a reasonable $2,000.00. Join the cutting edge of state-of-the-art mental health practice. Be prepared for prescription

privileges when they're eventually approved in your state.
New prescription privilege legislation has been introduced
in many states . . ."

After reading this, the disenchanted mental health worker,
used his already bulging credit card to finance the
continuing education course. While completing the course,
he read in a local trade publication: "The Mental Health
Prescription Privilege Bill was defeated in his state with
little hope of reinstatement in the foreseeable future."
Realizing that his financial mess has just gotten worse, the
wishful professional was even more discouraged.

Having wished his way into his decision, his 'common
sense' abandoned him because he reasoned with his heart
and not with his head. By suspending rational decision
making, his neediness colored his thinking. Retrospectively,
how could he have thought that responding to an ad meant
that he was on the threshold of salvaging his sagging
practice? He felt duped and eventually fleeced. As we've
seen, 'common sense' involves understanding the
repercussions of certain decisions. By drowning himself in
his own woes and consuming himself with his own
neediness, he failed to see that the light at the end of the
tunnel was a moving train.

The key to mastering common sense is divorcing yourself
just enough from your own problems so that you can look at
the situation more objectively. Opening your eyes can be a
shocking experience but it's also a good reality-check. Most
people don't dive into an empty swimming pool largely
because they're taught to look before they leap. When
confronted with 'attractive' propositions, it's difficult to sort
out good opportunities from bad ones. Reminding yourself
that if something looks too good to be true then it probably
is, is a beginning first step in protecting yourself from

unfounded optimism or misleading offers. It's helpful to ask yourself a simple question about the odds: What are the *real* chances that this will take place?

By thinking in terms of realistic chances, misleading and deceptive propositions can be avoided in most cases. It's also quite helpful before going off half-cocked, to check out the desirability of uncertain opportunities with disinterested people--those not having a material or emotional interest in the transaction. This certainly provides a better reality-check than anyone connected with promoting the proposition. As you can well imagine, asking a waitress what's good on the menu is risky business. Finding disinterested parties to give honest feedback helps make more informed decisions and provides at least some immunity against making costly mistakes.

Diplomacy

Without developing healthy diplomatic skills, otherwise easy to solve problems become far more complicated. Using a healthy dose of diplomacy assures--if nothing else-- that you'll create more warmth and openness in your audience. By couching things in language that softens the impact, new and otherwise unappealing propositions can be made more palatable. Telling it like it is, or blasting people with the unattractive aspects of whatever the situation, only invites defensiveness and breeds opposition. When new ideas are stated diplomatically they're more easily digested, despite the fact that the ideas themselves might be equally demanding or objectionable.

Diplomacy is really just presenting things in ways which circumvent objections--something good salespeople know instinctively and do automatically. By learning to communicate potentially onerous information in more acceptable ways, you'll be in a better position to orchestrate your agenda. An oblique, more camouflaged approach is usually preferred to simply beating someone over the head with your demands. Asking yourself: What can I do or say which will make the other person feel better about themselves? If your eye is trained on fulfilling this promise, many otherwise insurmountable situations are made much easier.

Sam, a mildly successful life-insurance salesman, is always looking for ways to 'close' his clients. Having been trained in the EST [the 'direct,' quick-fix approach growth seminar] school of human relating, he frequently delivers both barrels to his clients. In a recent sales presentation with his busy pressured attorney-client, he says:

"Look Bill, it's really quite simple. You either take this 10 year guaranteed renewable and level-term policy . . . OR you leave your wife and kids fully exposed to any untimely death. Now you wouldn't want to do that would you?"

Feeling a little beat up and boxed into a corner, his client responds defensively:

"Sam, I know I need to make a decision, but frankly I've got so much on my plate right now, I just can't make any decisions."

Again, coming from the confrontational school, the straight-shooting insurance salesman responds:

"Bill, don't be selfish! We'd all like to believe we're going to live forever. I don't blame you for wanting to bury your head in the sand. But, let's face it, we never know when the grim reaper's going to show up. You really have to accept the fact that you just can't ignore this responsibility."

Feeling even more turned off, Bill remarks:

"Sam, I'm just not ready to make this commitment right now. My wife keeps talking about wanting to buy a new car and go on a trip. I'll call *you* when I'm ready to look at this situation sometime in the near future." Leaving the sales meeting dejected, Sam might be ready to take a searching inventory of his sales strategy.

Believing incorrectly that the high-pressure sales approach yields the most fruit, Sam inadvertently shot himself in the foot. By being overly confrontational, our wannabe closer is once again oblivious to why he didn't walk away with the check. On closer inspection, he antagonized his ambivalent client by confronting him with his real fears: Whether he could (a) afford to subsidize his wife's extravagance *and* (b) make monthly payments on a life insurance policy.

Both of these sources of concern were enough to kill any deal, especially about a purchase in which he doesn't stand to gain any tangible personal benefits. If the salesman were showing more diplomacy and feeding his client what he wants to hear, he might have stood a better chance of walking away with that elusive check. Reconsidering the errors of his ways, he starts over and takes another stab at the sale:

"Bill, please forgive me for taking time out of your busy schedule. I'm well aware of how much you have on your plate. As you know, the last time we talked, you asked me to find you and your family that extra safety net. This level and guaranteed renewable term policy should do the job. Perhaps the timing for this isn't good right now. Not everyone has the presence of mind and sensitivity to think of their families. If this makes sense and gets the job done, then we can get this started right away for the amount seen on the policy."

Rather than displaying a confrontational style, the salesman is almost self-effacing by asking for forgiveness for taking up some of his time. This automatically makes a difficult discussion more acceptable. His validation of how much Bill has going on also shows deference to his busy schedule and time constraints. But more importantly, it shifts the balance of power onto the salesman, who's now in a more likely position of picking up that precarious check.

By almost showing indifference to making the sale and even suggesting that the timing might not be right, the salesman has cleverly positioned his client nearer to the close. Notice the hint of 'reverse psychology,' a soft but subtle and effective sales technique. We may never know whether Sam went home with the check, but it almost goes without saying that his second effort was preferred over the first one. Although it's tempting to try to impose your agenda on someone else, in most situations it engenders defensiveness and pushes doable sales out of reach. When frustrated and impatient, try a measured and tolerant dose of diplomacy.

Diplomacy is a calculated strategy by which considerable restraint is used to secure results not otherwise attainable. Rather than directly stating your case, simply use a little finesse with your words to get the job done. While we'd all like to say, "Just do it!," we need to recognize the fact that not everyone responds to this type of provocation. In most situations, couching your demands in more digestible language goes a long way:

- "I wonder if it's possible . . . ," or

- "Could I trouble you for . . . ," or

- "Please forgive me for asking . . . ," or

- "Would you kindly . . . ," or

- "I truly regret any inconvenience but . . . ," or

- "If it's not too much trouble, would you mind . . . ," etc.

By prefacing remarks with considerate statements like these, it's possible to transform ordinarily oppositional responses into ones more cooperative. Disguising personal demands or selfishness and creating the impression that you're oriented around serving the needs of others, opens many doors for individuals seeking expanded influence and persuasive power. Although it seems difficult, with a little awareness and practice, otherwise impossible demands can be changed into gracious concessions. Diplomacy is really much more about the *style* in which demands are being made, rather than the actual imposition. When pushing too hard and pressure fails to yield results, trying the *high-level intangible* of diplomacy expands your charisma and persuasive power.

Timing

Timing isn't just about kismet or the luck of the stars, it's about a more careful appraisal of when it's appropriate to pounce on an opportunity. Although some lament the fact that they're not at the right place at the right time, an appreciation of the circumstances goes a long way in pulling off otherwise untenable deals. After all, making the best presentation at the wrong time, simply won't compensate for the fact that you can't force something to take place. Picking your moments carefully demonstrates methodical planning which, in most instances, pays off better than just winging it.

Most opportunities don't just arise arbitrarily. While they appear spontaneous to some, more careful examination yields the fact that methodical calculation entered into the picture. To this extent, timing requires a careful appreciation of the circumstances which precede and follow any potential deal. Whether you're negotiating a car, selecting the right classes, buying a piece of jewelry or asking someone out on a date, increased awareness of the circumstances affecting the transaction should pay handsome rewards. If no such considerations are made, then one can expect constant disappointments with the faulty conclusion that the person has 'bad luck.' Once again, while it's better to be lucky than good, the truth is that it's better to be lucky *and* good. Showing competency with timing requires that individuals carefully plot out their best moments and fire their best shots.

A pleasure yacht broker, Joe, is always--or so it seems-- beat out on numerous deals. His clients are constantly disappointed over his failure to close deals for them, even when they seem so routine. This time is no exception, with his client insisting that they make a seller a low-ball offer. Although the agent knows the yacht is fresh on the market and the seller has not yet completed his transaction on the purchase of his new boat, he, once again, follows his client's demands. Discussing the offer with the seller's broker, Joe, says:

"Sam, I know this offer is about 25% below your asking price, but I can assure you my buyers are well qualified.

You know, 'A bird in the hand is worth two in the bush,' and although the offer might not be what you'd like . . . hey, it's at least an offer."

After receiving the offer, the seller's broker is reluctant to rain on Sam's parade, but sheepishly confesses:

"Sam, I'd love to present this offer to my client. But, as you can well imagine, they'd bite my head off. I promised them I wouldn't bother them with anything unreasonable-- or, at least to my client, that means within 10% of the asking price."

Now, had the buyer's broker been a little cognizant of timing, he might have asked the seller's broker something like:

"Sam, when do you expect your client to close the transaction on his new boat?"

After learning this, the buyer's broker would have a better sense realizing that the seller might entertain less attractive offers once he's the proud owner of two boats and paying twice the dock and maintenance fees. By analyzing the circumstances and delaying the presentation of the offer until after the purchase of the new boat was completed, the seller might be considerably more flexible about the price. While timing isn't everything, wouldn't it make a lot more sense to calculate the optimal point at which to make your best move?

As much as overly impulsive behavior can kill a deal, so too can excessive equivocation. Hesitating a little too long can also hurt your cause, especially when decisive action is required to complete a transaction. When you're too mired in minutia and blinded from looking at the overall picture, it's difficult to act decisively. Delaying decisions because of your own anxiety and compulsive need for reassurance, also plays havoc on successful deal-making. While looking before you leap has its place, you also have to know when it's time to pounce on a good opportunity.

A married couple had been endlessly searching for a signed lithograph by their favorite artist. For more than 10 years they'd been looking for the same piece they once saw in a famous gallery which exhibited the artist. While they were tempted at that time to purchase the work, they just couldn't make up their minds. The piece is now double the price. Finally, their arduous search was over. They found a private party with the piece at a price they could afford and were now ready to make their purchase. At the home of the seller, after examining the lithograph, his wife says:

"Sam, isn't it wonderful! We've finally found our lost jewel. Let's write the gentleman a deposit and pick it up tomorrow."

Her husband, always the circumspect type, says:

"You know Sally . . . it's really great! We're so lucky to have finally found it. But before I commit to it, let's go home and measure the spot in the living room where we intend to hang it. I'll feel a lot more comfortable about giving him a check once I know how it's going to fit."

After going home and taking the measurements, Sam was reassured and called back the seller the next morning. Getting through on the phone with the seller, he said:

"Hi Mr. Jones! This is Sam--you remember, the one who almost wrote you the check last night. I'd like to make arrangements to pay you and pick up the work."

Much to his shock, Mr. Jones said:

"Sam, it's good that you called. Unfortunately, right after you left another person came by unexpectedly, paid me cash on the spot, and already took the piece away. Sorry!"

All Mr. Jones could hear was a barely audible gulp on the other end of the line. By equivocating, Sam blew yet another opportunity. Needless to say, the couple were both ready to 'kill' each other. When it comes to timing, you have to know when to hesitate and when to act. By knowing in advance what it is you want and determining your own wishes, otherwise self-defeating inaction can be avoided. Like anything else, seizing the moment and the opportunity takes confidence in knowing clearly what you want.

Perhaps this is nowhere better illustrated than with timing involved in romantic relationships. How many times has the 'love of your life,' slipped out of your hands when you were just not ready? No matter how perfect the match, if someone's not prepared to make commitments, then even the best relationship can go down the tubes.

A hard-working, attractive 21 year old woman found the man of her dreams. At the time they met, he was about 1 year away from completing his college degree. They were madly in love and had everything in common: family backgrounds, shared values, interests, activities, food, etc. There was only one minor problem, Kevin wasn't ready for a commitment. He just felt he couldn't make any long-term promises when he didn't yet know what he'd be doing after graduation. He explained to Marge:

"Honey, you know how much I love you. You're the best! I couldn't be happier. Let's just keep things on hold until I graduate next year and then we can sit down and discuss our future plans."

Marge, always the pistol but trying her best to show some patience, was anxious to get on with her life. In her mind, what difference did it make whether Kevin made the commitment now or when he graduated? She'd given him everything without holding back--especially herself. Although he tried to explain himself and reason with her, she still felt rejected. Sharing some of her thoughts, she said:

"Kevin, your a great guy! We have a fantastic relationship. You're everything I've always wanted. But, you can't expect me to put my life on hold because you can't make up your mind. You know what I have to give you. All I'm asking you to do is to make a commitment now so I can start planning for the future. Is that really too much to ask?"

Needless to say, Kevin still wasn't ready to make that commitment and Marge wasn't prepared to put her life on hold. Shortly thereafter, Marge broke up the relationship. Years later, after Marge was divorced with two young daughters and Kevin was married in a stable relationship, Marge was kicking herself asking a nagging but honest question: Had she waited the year until Kevin graduated, would their relationship have worked out? Although we may never know that answer, it's clear that Marge's lack of flexibility and poor timing cost her the 'love of her life.' Had she shown more deliberation and calculated her moves more methodically, all her great expectations might have had a chance. While it appears that timing is locked into some divine kismet, the truth is that it's possible to time situations with greater precision. With a little more planning and a little less impatience, otherwise untenable situations can be made to work.

Awareness and Insight

Awareness is a special kind of insight which stems from tuning-in to your surroundings. Although it appears automatic, it actually involves the labor-intensive job of focusing your attention on essential aspects of your environment. It's about sizing up a situation just enough so you have a good sense of what's going on. Without awareness, it's like a bull walking through a china shop: You have no clue what's happening or what impact you're having in a delicate situation.

There's no one path to expanding awareness. And circuitous detours like digesting mind-altering chemicals or going on weekend retreats are no guarantee that you're going to 'get it,' regardless of what 'it' is. Awareness is much more related to understanding the many variables influencing a situation, whether it's in business or everyday life.

There's a special but surprising relationship between information and awareness. Having command of all the facts doesn't itself assure that a person will develop the insight they're seeking. How many times have you had all the information at your disposal, but somehow just didn't 'get it?' Clearing out certain misleading beliefs or unwarranted assumptions might be necessary before that vast reservoir of information can be used to orchestrate your agenda.

Continuing to put on the blinders because of powerful emotions--like fear, anger, guilt or even intense love--can prevent you from using valuable information. The old lament, 'I should have known better,' usually means that you had plenty of information and knew better, but somehow blind-spots prevented you from making the right decision. Sweeping out the blind-spots is easier said than done, but first begin with the awareness that powerful emotions can torpedo your efforts.

A wannabe actress with marginal success--but excellent acting talent--is known to sometimes upend herself by displaying overt animosity toward certain female casting directors. Although she normally has good social skills and understands the game, her cordiality is stretched to the breaking point when dealing with certain, middle-aged bleached-blond casting agents. A producer friend, with whom she's shared some of her 'dark' side, has painfully watched her sabotage her career and takes her aside:

"Marilyn, please forgive me for sounding a little blunt, but I've seen you audition for many parts and I can attest to the fact that you're an outstanding actress and deserved many of the parts. It breaks my heart to see you constantly shooting yourself in the foot. You've really got to learn to control your mouth!"

Hearing her concerns and reacting a little defensively, the talented but oblivious actress says:

"You know Angela . . . I really do appreciate your concerns, but let's face it, some of these casting directors act like princesses. You know how sensitive I am to most people. Since when have you known me to be sarcastic or hostile?" I'm actually one of the nicest people you'll ever meet. You really think I'm self-destructive?"

Wanting to respond but recognizing Marilyn's sensitivities, the producer replies:

"Marilyn, I think I know the problem. Some of these casting directors bear a striking similarity to your

MOTHER. They're middle aged, bleached-blond . . . and very CRITICAL! Do you think it's possible that you're expressing some unconscious anger toward them when it really belongs to your mother? My shrink is always telling me that's what I do!"

Appearing like she's been harpooned, Marilyn reacts:

"You know . . . I think you're on to something. Those casting agents do seem to resemble my mother--and, as I've shared with you, my mother is not my biggest fan. She's never had anything good to say about my acting or anything else for that matter. I guess I really do still have anger towards my MOTHER!"

Our savvy young actress knows the game of ingratiating herself to the appropriate people. She also knows what to do if she's really interested in landing parts. Behaving in hostile ways toward individuals capable of casting her is totally inconsistent with what she wants. Her lack of awareness blinded her from seeing how she'd been sabotaging her own chances of success. Although she had all the information, namely, she had talent, knew her lines and how to play the game, she lacked the *awareness* to advance her career. Paying closer attention to how repressed, unconscious emotional states can throw a roadblock in your way, should open many doors now tightly shut.

Awareness comes in many packages. Without looking for supreme revelations, it's most pragmatic and useful form is *self-awareness*. Although it's sometimes painful to look at one's limitations, it's also important to know your weaknesses to fully capitalize on your strengths. If you were aware of the fact that your personality comes off too strong, then wouldn't it make sense to try to tone yourself down? On the other hand, if you knew that your shyness or passivity hurts your chances, wouldn't that also be a great cue to increase your assertiveness and energy level? Actually, awareness isn't some magical property requiring trips to the psychic--or even the psychiatrist. It simply involves focusing on yourself, identifying your feelings, developing some self-awareness, and then changing your behavior to match the needs of a particular situation.

For some, the most difficult kind of awareness involves accepting feedback from others. When you consider what a terrific shortcut this can be, you'd think people would be waiting in line to receive candid feedback. For most people, it doesn't work that way. No, honest feedback can be quite threatening and even deflating to one's ego.   Although accepting constructive criticism is a tough pill to swallow, it can be the shortest distance to your goal.

Be grateful when someone thinks enough of you to share their perceptions--critical or otherwise. Try your best to use constructive feedback--no matter how painful it seems--to develop better self-awareness to improve your chances of success.   Remember, even the best, most insightful feedback--given by the best and brightest professionals for whom you're paying exorbitant fees--is an opinion. You don't have to be bludgeoned or deflated by someone's perceptions, especially when they don't match your own views. Just take it for what it's worth: An opportunity for self-improvement.

When a significant discrepancy exists between your own self-awareness and the views of disinterested others, e.g., 'I'm shocked that you think that about me,' try to resolve this difference not by dismissing it out of hand, but by stretching yourself to see-- even the remote possibility--that there might be some truth to what the other person is seeing.

Although criticism is difficult to stomach, it's a great opportunity to refine your high level intangibles. Without some openness to criticism--regardless of how it's delivered--it's difficult to learn new things. Arrogance, pretense, conceit, detachment and self-grandiosity are incompatible with personal growth and developing charisma.

A corporate executive in the steel industry is constantly replacing his middle management staff. Either by summary dismissals or abrupt terminations, he can't retain loyal and stable staff. Although appearing as a blowhard exterior, his personal assistant knows his more sensitive parts. Unfortunately for the rest of his staff, no one else has seen anything other than his arrogance, perfectionism, demandingness and abundant criticism. After a recent exodus from his division, he shares his frustrations with his assistant:

"Julie, I'm absolutely disgusted with the high turnover we've been having. For Christ's sake, what do you have to do to retain these junior executives? They're all prima donnas! When I started in this business, I remember my father saying, 'Son . . . just do your job and keep your mouth shut--when you're out of line, I'll let you know.' All these cry-babies want is to be told how wonderful they are. You know what, they're getting well-paid and that should be enough."

When his tirade had finally finished, his assistant thought she might have a chance to give him some long awaited feedback. Summoning all her diplomatic skills, she said:

"Mr. Appleton, you're a wonderful man! I've been the luckiest secretary in the world to have you as my boss. Your brilliant ideas are known by everyone. It sounds like your father was overly harsh with you. Although he didn't believe in 'ata-boys,' a lot of younger people need the validation from an approving parent. Maybe you're still carrying around some left over feelings from your father? What do you think?"

Appearing somewhat startled by her brazen but gentle confrontation, he reacted:

"Julie, I'm not paying you to be my shrink! God knows, I have a lot of unfinished feelings toward my father. Do you really think I've been overly harsh with my employees?"

Seizing the moment, sensing that Mr. Appleton was finally engaged in some healthy self-reflection, she carefully followed up on her thoughts:

"When you've asked me to do exit-interviews with your junior managers, the most common theme was that you constantly criticized and seldomly praised them. Many of them said that no matter what they did, it was never good enough."

Seeming somewhat startled and reacting to his assistant's feedback, Mr. Appleton shared his consternation:

"I can't believe people see me that way! When you give someone a chance, what better vote of confidence is there? Oh Julie, about my father, I think you're onto something. I really don't recall him ever saying anything positive to me. I just worked hard, dealt with his complaints and tried to find a silver lining. Do you think it's really possible that I've been taking out my unresolved anger toward my father on my middle managers? I guess I didn't have the best modeling. If that's true, I haven't had a clue."

Now, that's quite an insight considering Mr. Appleton's behavior has been so unconscious and habitual. By creating a little awareness about how his 'unfinished business' toward his father might have hurt his relationships with his own employees, Mr. Appleton was finally 'getting it.' Although old habits don't die easily, his awareness of his own 'stuff' and the manner in which he treated his past employees, seemed to be ringing a bell. While awareness like this comes and goes, it pays to be more in charge of the way you interact with people.

By riding herd on how you impact others, you're in a far better position to orchestrate your agenda. In Mr. Appleton's case, insoluble personal problems were directly linked to his abysmal self-awareness and his own loss of emotional control. Displacing repressed conflicts on unrelated bystanders might provide temporary relief but is a dangerous activity for individuals chasing the rainbows of success. As you can see, learning to stay in-charge and methodically influence others, first begins at home. While it's sometimes painful to accept the critical feedback, it's a small price to pay for redirecting an otherwise loose cannon. Accept it, embrace it, and, yes, welcome it, even when it hurts.

Politeness and Manners

In developing high-level intangibles related to charisma, there's no substitute for politeness and good manners. Regardless of how you disagree or how ludicrous you think others' opinions, learning to show unconditional respect is a tall order to fill. Abrasiveness and insensitivity have no place in the lives of charismatic individuals. While some operate under the illusion that they must step on people to attain success, the truth is you must learn the refined talent of walking more softly.

Stepping on too many feet clearly invites animosity,
making the road to success more treacherous. No matter
where you find yourself on the ladder, it pays to remember,
'As above, so below.' While not obvious, the principle is
clear: Treat all individuals whether they're parking your car
or negotiating a million dollar deal with the same
unconditional respect and the world will beat a path to your
door. 'As above, so below,' is an essential formula for
success. When you're too impressed with 'high altitude,'
that is, hobnobbing or rubbing elbows with the high-and-
mighty, you fail to see the importance of keeping your feet
planted on the ground. Some people lose sight of the fact
that the path to success crisscrosses many different
neighborhoods. Finding yourself too snobby or elitist to
fraternize with the many ostensibly unimportant but
significant contributors to your success, fails to recognize
the fact that everyone along the road to success plays an
important role.

Playing the military game in which you display
unquestioned obeisance to those above but contemptuous
disregard for those below, is a prescription for interpersonal
failure. While it's tempting to show respect only to those
perceived with power, money or authority, you never know
who's ultimately responsible for your biggest breaks.
Attesting to the unpredictability of life, your worst enemy
can turn out to be your best friend. It's certainly not
uncommon to receive help from unexpected sources. As a
good rule of thumb, make as many friends as possible on
your way up or down the mercurial escalator of success.
Don't burn *any* bridges.

By showing politeness, good manners, and courtesy to all
individuals, you don't have to make dramatic adjustments
along the way to the top. When interacting with people--
regardless of their status--find creative ways to make

someone feel special and valued. Dishing out compliments cost the same as delivering stinging criticisms. You'd think that knowing this would empower individuals to be more generous with their praise and compliments. And yet, like the troubled steel executive cited in the previous section, most people are more comfortable with negativity--it may be all they've ever known.

A presidential candidate is rounding the gun-lap in what seems like an interminable campaign: He's now in a make or break nationally publicized television debate with the incumbent president. The incumbent has hit him with a hail of denunciations and an avalanche of criticism. He's been misquoted, misspoken, and accused of everything short of being a hot-headed maniac. In one of the more heated exchanges, the incumbent says:

"Mr. O'Malley's economic plan would cause 30% inflation within one year and bankrupt our country. Even his tax cut proposal is clearly inflationary. And his own running mate-- when he was running for president--has called his plan 'voodoo economics,' and he's cited a very distinguished economist. Mr. O'Malley's propensity toward using military force could drag the U.S. into another world war. Other than that, I actually like Mr. O'Malley."

Still smiling broadly and shaking his head, the presidential candidate is asked whether he cares to respond. Keeping his cool, he says:

"Yes, I'd like to respond, very much. Please forgive me, Mr. President, for taking exception to your views. Your comments are, of course, a misstatement of my position. I sometimes think it's like a witch doctor who gets mad when a good doctor comes around with a cure that'll work."

Showing politeness and a little humor in the face of adversity and not stooping too low by engaging in comparable attacks, shows class and good breeding. Launching into vituperative counterattacks have the uncanny propensity of boomeranging--and to this exact extent, it's counterproductive. While enduring humiliation and punishment, try a measured dose of diplomacy with buoyant humor. Allowing your opponent the opportunity to attack and deflecting that attack with a cheerful but decisive response, has the effect of discrediting the opposition. Responding in-kind only amplifies your competitor's credibility by legitimizing the attack. As illogical as it sounds, if you counteract, their attack must have been warranted. Formulating a 'polite' and 'well mannered' response carries much more weight than getting down and dirty.

A marquee baseball player has been responsible for resuscitating a moribund franchise known more, in recent years, for foot-long hot dogs than championship baseball. Since his arrival he almost independently engineered the franchise's recovery from mediocrity. After 5 dedicated seasons, his agent is unable to negotiate an acceptable long-term contract. With trade rumors in the wind, he's approached by a reporter who says:

"Joe, we've heard rumors that you're on your way out of town. You must feel totally sold down the river by the new team management. What are your real feelings now about the current team management?"

Containing himself for months, the ball player is eager to finally respond:

"I just want all the fans to know how grateful I am to have played in this great city. There are no better fans in the world. As for the current management, obviously we would have liked to have worked out a deal. But they've [team management] made a business decision and we'll just have to live with it."

Not satisfied with a politically correct response, the reporter takes another swipe:

"Joe, let's face it, most of the press believe the management pulled the rug out from underneath you. Almost everyone thinks they dealt from the bottom of the deck."

Tempted to lash out at team management, the ball player takes a more philosophical approach and says:

"I know how disappointed many people are with the current circumstances. We wish it could have turned out differently. But this organization gave me a great opportunity to show my stuff--and I'll always be indebted to it. They [management] know what's best for their organization. After all, when it comes down to it, I'm just another employee. I'm sure they're looking out for their best interests just as we are."

Regardless of the provocation, it takes much more restraint to politely take exception to another's views. Side-stepping your true feelings requires a lot more finesse than unloading your frustrations. Venting your spleen only provides short-term relief and causes a number of unwanted side-effects. While it's tempting to engage in controversial attacks, it's far more beneficial to keep your options open by showing more restraint over your mouth. Because your 'worst enemy' can wind up your best friend, showing politeness and good manners leaves you with more leverage. When you burn your bridges--in whatever arena--you're narrowing your options and compromising future situations. With the 'small world' concept in which many people know each other via various kinds of networks, it only makes sense that relationships need to be nurtured rather than inadvertently torpedoed.

Politeness and goods manners helps assure that you're less vulnerable to attacks by others.   As we observed in DODGING THE BULLET, avoiding negativity, remaining positive and upbeat, displaying high energy and enthusiasm, showing grace under pressure, and keeping a good sense of humor, enables otherwise mortals to *Teflon*-coat their personalities.   By showing people the highest regard and treating them in a manner consistent with how you'd like to be treated, charisma will flow abundantly.

Energy and Motivation

Motivation and energy are essential fuels that drive the engines of charisma.   They're the explosive nucleus by which high-level intangibles are transformed into abundance and success.   On the other hand, bad energy, or negativity, generates   counterproductive forces unleashing dangerous riptides, leading to disappointment and failure. Without abundant positive energy and motivation, the best laid plans lose their 'snap, crackle and pop.'   While other elements of charisma can be missing or incomplete, without energy and motivation all else becomes irrelevant. Although for the lucky ones energy is in abundant supply, many people find themselves endlessly searching for--and never finding--this precious fountain of ambition and success.

Naturally occurring energy bubbles up from one's life or sexual force.   Like a volcanic hot spring, there are many elements affecting it's intensity and flow.   At times it's brimming over, and at other times it seems drained like an old battery. Consider for a moment your motivation in the presence of someone to whom you're sexually attracted. Without any effort, you come alive and you're vibrating like a tuning-fork, animated with endless conversation, intoxicated with intense emotions and buzzing with passion.

Without attraction and sexual energy, a person is like a wax dummy--lifeless and devoid of energy. To further your ambitions, this priceless commodity must be harnessed, channeled and directed toward your goals, not dissipated in various forms of indulgent behavior. Whether it's selling cars, negotiating business deals, persuading juries, canvassing votes, developing romances or any other activity in which you seek to orchestrate your agenda, energy and motivation must be abundantly supplied. When the energy is low, an otherwise intelligent and ambitious individual looks disinterested, tired and bored. Exuding high energy is your best defense against appearing depressed and unappealing.

Many people feel uncomfortable allowing this sexual/life-force to permeate their work and play. When someone has it, you immediately know it and sense its vibration. Regardless of 'what' they say, they're infinitely more 'interesting' and stimulating than their well informed but lifeless and boring counterparts. Allowing this powerful essential component of high-level intangibles to infiltrate your work will jump-start any goal or ambition. Sexual energy is clearly one of the core ingredients in your secret potion of charisma. While it's no guarantee of success, it delivers the added torque to help achieve your goals. Without it--whatever you do--you'll lack the pizzazz to reach your potential.

An attractive, ambitious, highly qualified, well-trained but chronically unemployed executive is having a nightmare of a time trying to land another position. Interview after interview, she finds herself thoroughly frustrated opening up the 'We regret to inform you . . .' letters. She has no clue what she's doing wrong. Attributing it to bad luck, she's beginning to develop some cryptic but unmistakable elements of paranoia. When speaking to her best friend she says:

"You know Sally [speaking slowly and making poor eye contact]. . . I just get the impression that these women are looking at me like I'm some type of street walker. I swear I can see them looking at me in 'funny' ways. My unemployment is due to run out next month. I just don't know what I'm going to do."

Expressing some concern, her girl friend comments:

"Jill, you seem like you've been under enormous stress. You look totally exhausted--drained of all your energy. Now I'm just guessing. If others are seeing what I'm seeing, maybe they think you're either depressed or bored."

Although somewhat surprised, her girl friend Sally remarks:

"You know . . . ever since breaking up with Bob, I just haven't been myself. I just can't find any energy to do anything, including interview for jobs."

Let's face it, if you're depleted of all your energy and trying to sleepwalk through job interviews or relationships, you're not going to have too much appeal. If you're running on fumes, burning the candles at both ends, showing signs of stress, exhaustion, and, yes, depression, then ignoring these warning signs can prove disastrous to your career or social life. When usurped of your energy, you have to find some way of getting it back. Dousing yourself with pots of Starbucks will only backfire by failing to deal with the short in your system. Regaining your equilibrium and restoring your energy might require consulting a professional specialized in managing stress and depression. Stress and depression are symptoms of life in the fast lane and can be managed quite effectively. But nothing can be done until you admit that you've got a problem.

An attractive, divorced, single parent account executive in the hosiery industry is having repetitive failures at her video dating service. Having already submitted to several cosmetic surgeries, her physician takes her aside and shares his thoughts:

"Judy, you're an attractive, highly intelligent gal. I know I can continue tinkering with your *appearance* but that's not-- at least as I *see* it--why you're not finding Mr. Right. I've noticed that you seem stressed, slowed down, low-energy and lacking *joie de vivre.*
I know that if I met you for the first time, I'd think you were distracted and bored."

Appearing a little surprised by her doctor's frankness but trying her best to digest his feedback, Judy remarks:

"Dr. Sanders . . . To tell you the truth, I don't know when I'm under stress. I've been living this way so long I don't know any different. Well, if you think this is hurting my chances of finding a relationship--I'm all ears. What do you suggest that I do?"

Pleased with her reaction but not wanting to alarm her, Dr. Sanders says:

"Your know Judy, after thinking about your case, I think you have a biochemical imbalance. There are a number of wonderful medications to correct this. They also have the effect of reducing stress and increasing your energy-level. I think I'm going to write you a prescription for Prozac--that should do to the trick."

When the life-forces ebb due to adverse life-circumstances and when it creates biochemical depletion, it certainly makes sense to seek professional help. But, in many instances, so called 'biochemical imbalances' are really more related to lacking enthusiastic interest in life or a failure to have important goals. All the pots of coffee, over-the-counter chemicals, prescription drugs, or any other gimmick won't restore a depleted *joie de vivre,* if the person doesn't take a searching inventory of their life.

Without a little introspection, by asking a simple but important question, 'What would make me happy?,' all the external cures or distractions will likely come up blanks. In Judy's case, it probably won't hurt to try Prozac. But it also wouldn't hurt to examine how her coping skills or ways of processing stress need some improvement. Whether she's actually 'depressed' is anyone's guess. But by engaging in chronic negativity, including whining, complaining, criticizing, withdrawing, ventilating, etc., that's as much of a turn-off to would-be suitors as anything else. Reminding yourself to recharge your sexual/life force and allow its appropriate and less inhibited expressions in your relationships at work and elsewhere, will go a long way in developing the charisma to advance your agenda.

Experience and Good Judgment

Profiting from experience is certainly a valuable lesson. Without it, individuals are forever doomed to make the same repetitive mistakes. Since the road to success is always under construction, there are many learning opportunities. But if individuals have difficulty learning from experience, it's going to be a very long and winding road. Some people are quick studies in that they make their share of mistakes but make needed corrections to achieve their goals. For others, learning from experience is a far more lengthy and arduous process. 'Quick studies' always want to get 'quicker' but those taking the more tortured path also have ways of reducing unnecessary mistakes and learning at a faster pace.

While some would argue that there are no short cuts in life, the basic premise of this book is that by tuning-in and paying closer attention to high-level intangibles--the basic elements of charisma--silly mistakes can be preempted and success is one definite step closer. By focusing on the elements of charisma and learning from the mistakes of others, it's possible to accelerate the learning process. Regrettably, many people don't know what prevents them from learning. Or, if they do know, they do their utmost to avoid facing their 'darker' side.

Although people say they want advice--whether paid for or not--they don't typically take it. Or, if they do take it, for whatever reason, it's not assimilated and used. Why? If learning something new is going to help your position, then why ignore it or reject it? It really doesn't make economic sense but it does make psychological sense. New learning is typically blocked by fear: Fear of the unknown; fear of change; fear of admitting that you're not in control of your life; or even fear that you're incapable of learning new things. Actually, there are many other fears as well.

To profit from experience you have to (a) admit you don't know everything, (b) concede you need all the help you can get, (c) become receptive to new suggestions, and (d) practice the new ideas to assure learning occurs. It's really that simple. Now, of course, your still wondering why some learn faster than others and some don't seem to learn at all. From our perspective, speed is less important than openness and receptivity. Speed will eventually follow once you're open and receptive to trying new and different ways. Who's really timing or scoring you? In most cases, it's only yourself.

A president of a prestigious graduate school has been warned not to antagonize anyone on the accreditation committee re-certifying their program. On a past occasion, a senseless argument--having nothing to do with the school's academic program--cost the school its accreditation for several months, throwing the faculty and student body into chaos. The argument stemmed from the chief auditor questioning the president's belt buckle which was an exotic, unused hash pipe. During the current accreditation meeting, the president--I guess trying to make a point--wore the same belt. Once again, the chief auditor digressed from his academic review and threw in his two cents:

"Mr. Cohen, can you tell me why you're wearing drug paraphernalia to our meeting? Does this reflect your institution's policy on drug abuse? Or, is this just your way of saluting me with your middle finger? I can't for the life of me figure out what you're getting at."

Having failed to profit from his last encounter, the school president went ballistic:

"You have no right to come to my school and accuse me of anything. You're here to evaluate our academic program not my choice of accessories. I think you're out of line--and I'm not going to take it anymore!"

Reacting to the president's ire, the chief auditor says:

"Mr. Cohen, with all due respect, I have every right to evaluate any aspect to your program, including the appropriateness or suitability to your administration and faculty. That's all within my legal authority. What's your authority to treat me like one of your students? I can't see any reason for continuing this evaluation any longer. As far as I'm concerned, this meeting is now over!"

The chief auditor packed up his briefcase and took off. The school temporarily lost its accreditation hurting the faculty and student body; and enrollment at the renowned institution precipitously dropped. All of this was caused by someone incapable or unwilling to profit from his prior experience. Why would anyone deliberately self-destruct, when he knew in advance what was expected of him? What was it that made the school president unable to benefit from the past experience which became a carbon copy of the current one? Since making the same mistakes is costly and can result in catastrophic damage to one's career or social standing, it only makes sense to learn to avoid the same predictable pitfalls.

The fact that severe ego-problems eclipse rational judgment and interfere with learning shouldn't come as a big surprise. Human learning isn't only based on information, memory and regurgitation. It's heavily dependent on personality factors--like the condition of one's ego--which either makes or breaks the learning process.

Although the president 'knew' better, he over-reacted and became provocative. His need to be right and to assert his will prevented him from seeing the rather dire consequences. As long as one is arrogant, haughty, grandiose and self-centered--regardless of one's high IQ--learning won't occur easily. If you already 'know it all,' what's left to learn?

It's equally difficult to talk about good judgment when acting like a loose cannon. If judgment is clouded by unconscious or conscious personality factors which either prevent profiting from experience or promote self-destructive behavior, then it's would seem time, once again, for some honest self-reflection.

Experience is an important intangible related to charisma when it's used to help perform or solve problems. If experience is poorly assimilated--for any reason--or if bad habits interfere with learning, then experience can't be regarded as a helpful high-level intangible. In most cases, 'having been there and done that' places individuals at a distinct advantage. For most people, with repeated exposure and practice, performance is greatly enhanced. Although this isn't always true, it's a good rule of thumb. But if doing the same old things brings you repeated heartaches and failure, you might have to also unlearn counterproductive ways.

When considering what constitutes 'good judgment' it involves making a choice--typically based on experience--which enhances the person's situation. While experience and good judgment usually go together, they don't always go hand in hand. Sometimes bad experiences, like traumatic events, hurt an individual's future performance. But when it comes to completing complex tasks--like bypass surgery--it pays to have experience under your belt. Although youth and experience have their place, most people find past experience an important high-level intangible and essential element of charisma.

Drive and Desire

Like energy and motivation, drive and desire are also essential high-level intangibles influencing charisma. It's finding and sustaining the drive that's difficult for most people. And yet those without drive or desire, sometimes spend a lifetime searching--and never finding--this coveted essence. Drive stems from many varied sources: For some it's a need for recognition and approval, while for others it's about money and fame. When drive originates from a need for wealth, it's often difficult to sustain since most individuals are seldomly motivated only by pots of gold. While roaming the path of success, fulfillment must also come from the satisfaction along the way--the process of achieving or doing. Nothing motivates like success itself. It pays to also like what you're doing!

External goals--with promises of wealth and its unending accouterments--are a powerful source of ambition to many individuals. This is especially true when people come from humble beginnings, watching from a distance and wishing for the trappings of the good life. Measuring their success against others living the promised life, their motivation for the fabled existence burns like a consuming flame. Yes, for the many victims of unfortunate beginnings or harsh economic times, they're permanently etched with an insatiable desire to pay their bills and attain affluence. Relentlessly pursuing their dreams for success, these same individuals possess an intense desire and lasting drive for success: Their motivation often stems from powerful fears of failure and poverty.

Once their goals are realized and they're no longer plagued with their old fears, only then do they sometimes experience the proverbial existential crisis of, 'Is this all there is?' While material success energizes drive for some, others find themselves chasing a different kind of reward. As elusive as it is chasing greenbacks, it's even more ethereal attempting to satisfy the unquenchable thirst for perfection. Burning with perfectionistic cravings, these individuals find no relief from unrealistic internal demands.

An entertainment superstar, having achieved success beyond anyone's wildest fantasies, finds himself always expecting more. Regardless of the accolades and adoration of untold millions, he's never quite satisfied with his accomplishments. Finally consenting to a rare interview, a renowned talk show host asks:

"Tell us Mr. Bellini: What's it really like to be a living legend? You're worshipped like a God by all your adoring fans!"

Taken somewhat aback by what he experiences as undue adulation, the superstar responds:

"You know . . . I don't really get what people mean by a legend. I'm just a hard worker. There's really nothing different about me than anyone else who's worked hard and enjoyed some success."

Providing a brief X-ray into the mind of those driven to push the envelope of human potential, it displays the impossibility of satisfying a relentless and unforgiving internal judge. Exceeding others' standards provides little relief to those exalting and suffering from their own perfectionism. Intensely motivated and driven individuals are often besieged with insatiable internal demands robbing them of the satisfaction and fulfillment they rightly deserve. It's a regrettable fact that many accomplished individuals are saddled with this unfair burden. Despite this onus, other individuals are cursed with a vacuum of such drive, leaving them drifting and floundering through life with little or no ambition.

As we've said, finding this drive or intense desire for success is easier said than done. Although some are blessed with all the motivation in the world, others suffer from the 'wannabe' and chronic procrastination syndrome, either living with mediocrity or drifting from one pipe-dream to another. For those looking to increase their drive, it's helpful to stake out challenging but doable goals. Fixing your sights too high, deflates drive and motivation by setting you up for predictable failure. Nothing usurps precious motivation more than repeated disappointment and failure.

At the same time, we shouldn't be setting the bar too low either since it breeds complacency and a phony sense of accomplishment. While it's comfortable to be a big fish in a small pond, it's also inherently dissatisfying. Having new challenges and goals is an essential part of maintaining your motivation for life. One is only too reminded of the failed promises of 'early' retirement in which normally occurring goals are no longer present. By setting new goals--at any stage of life--and pursuing them vigorously, the lost drive and ambition can be rediscovered.

A 75 year old physician facing his mortality and imminent retirement, whose contorted and atrophied body was ravaged by 50 years of smoking and inactivity, is stunned with the piercing revelation of investing in his own health. Like a glowing light, he's suddenly driven to undo his deteriorated condition and attain his own potential of fitness. Although he's been inactive for years, his goal is to run and win a 10K race. Slowly and painfully, inch by inch, he begins walking. After several months he picks up his pace, and finally begins to jog. Over a period of years he religiously conditions himself and ultimately competes in his first race. Surprising himself and all his naysayers, he continues to improve, work out by work out, race by race. He finally succeeds in winning his first 10K race and then others. At age 80, he hikes 22 miles to the summit of Mt. Whitney [alt.14, 495 ft.] and returns safely home the same day. He's exceeded all his goals but not his own expectations. While his colleagues are checking themselves into nursing homes, he continues to jog. Setting realistic and doable goals enabled him to regain his drive.

Interviewed by a reporter from a seniors publication, he's asked:

"What's your secret? How did you do it? Surely you wouldn't recommend your regimen to others."

Responding to the reporter's questions, the now 89 year old responds:

"On the last point, if they wanted their health as badly as I did, I could never discourage anyone from trying. You see . . . First, I harnessed my enthusiasm. Second, I set small but doable goals. And third, I worked hard and never quit. You'll see--if you set some goals and they're realistic, there's absolutely nothing that you can't do!"

Finding yourself devoid of elusive drive and desire, set some simple goals. Goals seem to create the structure in which achievement takes place. While some people find themselves on auto-pilot for their careers, that doesn't mean it's not OK for others to set specific goals. Whether the drive is internal (like the pursuit of perfection) or external (like making a million dollars) it doesn't really matter as long as it jump-starts your ambitions. After climbing the mountain and achieving your goals--no matter how inconsequential--take special time to reward yourself. After you celebrate and bask in your victory, just remember there are still other mountains to be climbed.

Charm, Class and Grace Under Pressure

Life is filled with pressure situations in business and elsewhere. It's not a matter of whether someone's going to be overloaded with stress and pressure, it's matter of when. How and what way you respond to pressure is another important high-level intangible associated with charisma. While some people 'crack' under the pressure, charismatic people--at least publicly--present a masterful facade. Rarely do you see them ranting and raving, going ballistic or engaged in intemperate displays. No, they do their best to remain charming despite the adversity. Nothing strips away charisma faster that exhibiting vulgar or revolting behavior.

For those chasing the magic of charisma, unflappable internal control enables one to present an idyllic image. They reserve the privilege of exposing their darker side, their moodiness, their outbursts, their internal fears, their perverted obsessions, their eccentric habits to only their special confidants and friends, like psychotherapists, publicists, agents, personal managers, spouses and others whose possible effect on their image is negligible. After all, charisma--or that magnetic personal power--is closely related to image. Although it can be difficult to create, it's easy to destroy. One hasty public display or episode in which the darker side is exposed, might be enough to short-circuit that special power. Because of its mercurial quality, charisma must be maintained with charm and finesse.

Charismatic people expose the public only to qualities which promotes their image.

Under the gun, when the heat is turned up, charismatic individuals perform their best because they're constantly seeking the approval and adulation of others. They respond best to challenges. When talking about 'approval ratings' that's really all that matters. Whether they're impressing their ministries, constituencies, boards of directors, the press or any other groups or individuals with whom they're scoring points, charismatic people are highly dependent on their audience. Without an audience, all their high-level intangibles and special talents fall on deaf ears. You can't get under the skin of a charismatic person by attacking them, for they're well equipped to manage any adverse circumstance. But you can begin to undermine their power by ignoring or shunning them. Ostracism or rejection is a fate worst than death.

A handsome, charming, nationally known athlete is accused of murdering his ex-wife and friend. Although acquitted of murder with the help of some gifted attorneys, his image has been irreparably damaged. Despite his protests, he's been abandoned by all his commercial endorsements. He's also been permanently ostracized from most of his business and social connections. After losing a civil judgment, his credibility has taken another irreversible hit. Despite all the heroic attempts of his publicity team, his charisma has been mortally wounded. During a recent interview, he's asked by a TV interviewer whether he's been unfairly treated:

"Oh, Absolutely. . . I can't tell you how much I appreciate you telling my side of the story. They [the prosecuting attorneys, detectives and police] fabricated all the evidence. My attorneys clearly showed I was framed. Why would anyone think I would kill the mother of my children? I've lost everything--my home, my career, my social life. What more do they want? I feel that I'm the victim!"

Demonstrating that he's still retained some of his charisma, conveys his gratitude to the interviewer which automatically puts her on the defensive. Turning the tables, he's now in the position of controlling the interview. Soliciting sympathy by seeing himself as the victim, also helps stave off more serious questions. True to his *Teflon* personality, he's still doing his best to avoid negativity and remain charming. But because his Teflon is frayed and his charisma is tarnished, he doesn't have the same persuasive powers as he once did. Despite all of the interviewer's pointed questions, he still doesn't lose control or go ballistic. He continues to show some charm, grace under pressure, and sticks to the same tired explanations.

As we've said, resorting to vulgarities and going ballistic is clear evidence that one's charisma has worn thin. Because charm and methodical control are essential high-level intangibles, when they're eclipsed by emotional outbursts it signals the demise of charisma. While charisma is a somewhat resilient quality, it can be stretched to the breaking point. Clearly, threatening charismatic people with a loss of approval or rejection takes it toll. Eventually, when faced with repeated rejection and disfavor, they begin to crack and exhibit classless behavior. Remember, despite all the humiliation and failure, charismatic individuals covet their pride and dignity. When sifting through the ruins of their careers or relationships, it's all they have left. When forced to endure sustained periods of shame, humiliation and rejection, they begin to exhibit uncharacteristic and irrational behavior.

A proud, patriotic and fiery congressman, known for his vituperation and ethnic insensitivity, finds himself upended in a recent election by a 'minority' candidate. Although his once ethnically homogeneous district has changed drastically, he didn't seem to keep pace. Months after his stunning defeat, he's faced with the unkind reality that he's been rejected by his constituency. A congressional committee examining his allegations of voter fraud has recently certified the election. His ordinary restraints are pushed over the edged. At a press conference, he's questioned by a contentious reporter:

"Mr. Brown, why is it that you can't seem to accept the fact that you were defeated fair and square in this election? Isn't it time for you to step aside and accept the will of people?"

Boiling over with fury, the congressman reacts:

"NO, NO, NO! I'll never concede this election. Everyone knows that my opponent stuffed the ballot boxes. I'm a decorated war hero. She's a nothing, a zero, a nobody and a phony. What does she know about politics? How could she possibly defeat me fair and square? It just couldn't happen. Engaging in fraud was her only way."

After his tirade subsided, the reporter pressed on his with case:

"Mr. Brown, I think the congress and public are well aware of your feelings. Isn't it time for you to accept the will of your district and 'graciously' step aside?"

Barely containing himself, the defiant congressman says:

"NEVER!"

Public displays of rage, fury, denunciations, attacks, accusations, etc., have the uncanny effect of boomeranging and unraveling charisma. Although righteousness displays a sort of conviction to one's beliefs, it's not a license to lash out at the world. Being stripped of his audience and rejected, the otherwise hot-headed congressman went over the top. After losing his long-shot bid to have the congress decertify the election, he went ballistic. Losing control and displaying intemperate behavior is totally incompatible with maintaining charisma or any other type of personal power. By taking the pressure without breaking down and resorting to name-calling and overt displays of rage, one is left in a far better position of salvaging a bad situation.

Exhibiting public tantrums and vulgarities usually backfires and comes back to haunt you. Regardless of all the wonderful things you've done in the past, the 'recency effect' guarantees that the last thing remembered will be the classless, uncouth behavior. If you're not retiring from the planet, it's quite conceivable that you'll still need others' support at some point in the future. Ugly episodes tend to burn bridges and necessitate adroit damage control strategies which have dicey results. Maintaining your dignity and class in the face of adversity is the best test of true charisma. Regardless of the provocation or adversity, don't lash out. Try a healthy dose of tact and diplomacy, it really works! By showing discipline and restraining your darker side, you'll be in a better position of eventually furthering your agenda.

Playfulness and Humor

Charismatic people openly pour themselves out in social situations: They fight the tendency toward detachment, aloofness and withdrawal. Despite public perceptions of power, prestige and occasional brilliance, they remain approachable by engaging in playful dialogue and conversation. Even when the pressure is heaped on, when they're under siege, and when their credibility and position is under attack, charismatic individuals prefer social dialogue over isolation and withdrawal. It's their willingness to hang-in-there and stay engaged in lively discussion that leaves the impression that they won't take no for an answer--that they'll never quit. This defiance and not accepting 'no' attitude is related to the fact that charismatic people have difficulty dealing with rejection: They handle it by essentially *not* dealing with it.

Overcoming objections or not accepting the negativity or rejections of others is one of their greatest strengths. Instead of accepting rejection, charismatic individuals prefer to remain engaged in energetic conversation, even when it seems they're not scoring points and facing failure. Although they want to win, it's the act of engagement or the 'staying in the hunt' which is kept alive. Whether charismatic people ultimately prevail is considered less relevant than remaining actively involved. The fact that they're able to keep their counterparts involved in animated talk consumes much of their interests. Charismatic individuals are acutely aware of the fact that if they maintain a playful dialogue and flirtation, they've got a good chance of eventually prevailing.

Tenaciously remaining engaged--in whatever they're doing--is actually less related to 'winning' or beating the opposition, than more intimately related to a fear of rejection. As we've said [see section on Drive and Desire], charismatic individuals aren't primarily motivated by money. Surprising as it seems, they're constantly seeking approval and recognition from others. Always comparing themselves and measuring their success against 'hypothetical' competitors, they usually find themselves in an interminable race for social approval.

Because of this consuming need, charismatic people are often seen as highly competitive and ambitious. Despite appearing competitive with external opponents, the truth is that they're competing with insatiable internal demands for acceptance and recognition. Like an unquenchable thirst, they crave approbation and rarely tire of it, regardless of how many awards and accomplishments they've accumulated. Show me a charismatic person who doesn't want approval and recognition and I'll show you someone who's been lowered six feet under. It's not in their nature to feel satisfied with any one accomplishment; since their hunger for attention and recognition knows no real limits.

A charismatic art history professor, whose personality and public lectures were considered legendary, is beginning a talk to an energetic audience about the flamboyant Spanish artist Pablo Picasso. Although he's frequently invited to lecture around the world and receives abundant accolades, his success has never gone to his head: Instead, he's down to earth, approachable and charming. At times, he's even known for making unexpected self-deprecating remarks. His self-effacing humor seems to endear him to his audience. While beginning a recent lecture, the professor commented:

"Thank you all for allowing me to, once again, cure your insomnia. Forgive me for boring you with another neurotic artist. My mission today is keeping you awake--among other things! Now let's spend a few minutes talking about Mr. Picasso . . ."

After the lecture ended, the audience was on its feet applauding his performance. Once again, his energetic delivery delighted the audience. Far from falling asleep, they were on the edges of their seats hanging on every word. His self-deprecating humor created a strange bond with the audience by setting them up for a sort of paradox: How could they do anything other than remain intensely focused on his lecture? Following the lecture, a member of the audience went up to him and asked:

"Mr. Semolina, this was another brilliant lecture. How do you keep yourself so pumped-up about the same subject year after year. Although I must have heard this one 5 times, it always seems like the first--where do you get all your enthusiasm?"

Responding to her comments, he says:

"Actually, it's very simple. Every new lecture I'm faced with the same dilemma. I can't rely on the applause I got the last time. I guess I'm always afraid that the applause won't be as loud the next time around--and that's what keeps me on my toes!"

Strange as it seems, the internal architecture of charismatic people is marked by insecurity and irrational fears of rejection and failure. As dynamic as Mr. Semolina seems to his audience, he sees himself in a different light. In order to compensate for his insecurity, he pushes himself to extraordinary levels every time he performs. His irrational fears of a lowered applause-meter, drive him to out do himself every time he lectures. It's not really that he possesses extraordinary new excitement about his subject; he's determined to regain that priceless but elusive approval he received the last time he performed. Does this sound like insecurity? You bet. But it underscores one of the hidden intangibles or essences seen in charisma: The insatiable need to reclaim the lost attention and approval one more time.

While self-effacing humor adds to charisma, so does flirtatiousness when engaging in social interaction. Charismatic people are rarely short on conversation, preferring instead to keep discussions going to eventually get their way. Using digression in clever ways, they're capable of swirling around various topics eventually returning to the key issues connected with their agenda. Whether it's making sales, canvassing for votes, soliciting intimacy or any other goal, charismatic people don't perform the 'mid-syllable chop' and break off communication! Conversations aren't abruptly ended simply because they've been distracted or lost interest. Instead, they're always focused on getting their way or advancing their cause. They know that if someone stops talking in most social situations, the probability of rejection increases dramatically. Finding creative ways of keeping conversations going is their best defense against possible rejection.

A personal injury attorney is under the gun trying to negotiate--with very little success--a settlement for an impatient client. Always priding himself on being a straight shooter, he doesn't hesitate to get down to business. Unfortunately, the last conversation with the insurance adjuster ended with the receiver crashing down on the other end of the line. Going *tete-a-tete* has resulted in very little progress with the adjuster finally saying, "We'll see you in court . . ." He decides to take a different tact and engage her in 'idle' conversation. In a more recent phone call he says:

"Hi Marge, it's Bill again. What's happening? It's been a about a month since we last spoke. I sure hope everything is going well with you. Do I recall hearing that you're engaged now. How's it going? I think that's really great!"

Taking the bait, Marge says:

"Bill, funny you should ask. Actually I was engaged, but that's ancient history now. I found out that his favorite pastime was putting coke up his nose. Can you image what I would've gotten myself into?"

Showing concern and reacting to her situation, the attorney says:

"Marge, that's really a shame. It shows you how little we actually know about people. What's really frightening is that had you not found out, you would've married him without any questions. You're really smart to have waited and gotten to know him a little better. I'm sure this was meant to be. When the situation's right, you'll know it. When you think of negotiating an annulment or divorce agreement, settling these accident cases is really a piece of cake!"

Appreciating Bills remarks, the adjuster says:

"You know Bill, you're absolutely right! Life's too short to nickel and dime each other about legitimate settlements when this other type of stuff is going on. Look, I know we've had our differences in the past, but you tell me what you think is reasonable and I'll do everything I can to make it happen."

Thrown for a loop, Bill reacts quickly:

"Marge . . . You're really going through a lot now. I didn't call you up with the intention of hitting you up at a bad time. Maybe this isn't the right time to be discussing a settlement. We're in no rush to settle this case, and, besides, your happiness is a lot more important to me than satisfying my client's demands. Take as long as you need to figure things out."

Finding Bill's comments sensitive and concerned, Marge says:

"No, really Bill--you're a doll! I can't tell you how special it makes me feel that you're concerned with my situation. Don't worry about it anymore. Just make me what you think is a reasonable offer and we'll finally put this one to rest. Really--it's no problem!"

Keeping the lines of communication open is far more desirable than finding yourself on the wrong end of a hang-up. Showing empathy with another person's situation and engaging in playful dialogue, enables an individual to remain playfully engaged when they were otherwise rejected. It follows a simple but powerful premise that tuning-in to the needs of others pays rich dividends. When the attorney decided to become less business-like and 'beat around the bush,' the adjuster felt cared about and wasn't on the defensive. No longer opponents facing-off on center ice, they were 'friends' openly talking and sharing personal information. Although this tactic doesn't work all the time, camouflaging your intentions and engaging in flirtatious, playful conversations, can be your ace in the hole.

Some Final Thoughts

High-level intangibles are those subtle but verifiable essences which contribute to an individual's charisma. When you skim off all the technical skills, they represent those magical but predictable ingredients responsible for success. Without these special talents, all the education, training and skills, can't rescue an individual whose high-level intangibles are poorly developed. While it's easy to wrongly pin these barely noticeable talents on luck, they're clearly labeled on their own. Paying close attention and developing these talents improves social effectiveness in many areas. Expanded charisma is an unmistakable consequence of improving high-level intangibles. When they're in gear, it makes success a whole lot easier.

Displaying overt aggression and showing intemperate emotional episodes dissolve charisma. By learning to calculate and plan one's responses, it's far easier to advance your agenda. Blasting people with demands and displaying 'brutal' honesty shows a lack of sensitivity and concern for others. While there's a premium placed on honesty, it's far more effective to express your views in non-offensive ways, even when you're shading or spinning the truth to spare someone's feelings.

Beating people up with your version of the truth is inherently problematic, since it creates the impression that you're insensitive and even offensive. Excessive opinionating runs the risk of alienating others and stripping off your charisma. It's far safer and more effective to allow someone to save face, rather than proving that you're always right. Ego problems have no place in the public lives of charismatic people. What occurs in private is another story.

Picking your moments and timing your moves are essential for success. Charisma involves a calculated risk of when it's right to seize the moment. Waiting too long or acting impulsively without good preparation, invites unnecessary failure. It pays to control impatience and wait until it's the right time to act decisively. At other times, by waiting too long you'll miss the boat.

Tuning in to the needs of others and knowing your effect on people, goes a long way in helping to achieve your goals. Failing to check-out the effect of your behavior risks alienating others and dilutes your charisma. Demonstrating politeness and good manners in the face of provocation and adversity shows the kind of class required for asserting personal power.

Showing high energy and enthusiasm--regardless of how beaten down you actually feel--are essential features of charisma. Appearing low energy, withdrawn or depressed, runs the risk of being seen as boring and lifeless. Charisma is conveyed by increasing your voltage whenever possible. When drive and desire are difficult to find, select realistic and doable goals which increase your chances of success. At the same time, don't undersell your ambitions.

While interacting with others, remain playful and show good humor whenever appropriate. An upbeat and cheerful disposition is always preferred over one more dour and devoid of humor. Although life has serious moments, don't be afraid to find the brighter side to adversity even where it's not obvious. Avoiding negativity--the tendency toward lashing out--and displaying a playful attitude, goes a long way in attaining otherwise unlikely goals. Keeping the dialogue going, despite all of the attempts by others to break it off, helps orchestrate your agenda.

Remain resolute in your commitment to multiply the good fortune and success of others. Resist the misguided and counterproductive temptation toward selfishness. Contrary to what it seems, self-centeredness is a poison pill to charisma and a prelude to failure. By placing your needs in the back-seat and doing your utmost to help others, the waves of success will move in your direction. Just as surely, if you place yourself first, you may very well wind up last.

Points to Remember

- Use savoir fair, tact, and face-saving measures at all times

- Incorporate 'common sense' into your interactions

- Display high levels of diplomacy while relating to others

- Calculate your timing with precision before making your moves

- Demonstrate good awareness of and insight into yourself and others

- Show politeness and good manners at all times

- Exhibit high levels of energy and motivation

- Learn from experience and show good judgment

- Develop and sustain high levels of drive and desire

- Reflect charm, class and grace under pressure when facing adversity

- Engage in playful conversations and show good humor whenever possible

Chapter 2

NARCISSISM
ON THE ROPES

In this chapter you'll learn about the complex relationship between charisma and narcissism. • Introduction • Putting a lid on grandiosity • Empathy pays its weight in gold • Stop looking in the mirror • Co-dependency 'some more' Arrogance, ignorance and stupidity • Embracing altruism Some final thoughts • Points to remember

Introduction

Narcissism--the cultural attitude or trend of extreme self-centeredness--is a poison pill to the fragile commodity of charisma. It's a self-destructive *low-level* intangible which writes an imminent obituary for eventual failure. While it's true that many charismatic people *appear* vain and egocentric--and they certainly do--it's also true that they're actually oriented around meeting the needs of others. Whether it's a politician, corporate executive or professional athlete, the altruistic promises are always the same: Follow me or my leadership and allow me to help improve *your* situation. Personal interests are strategically placed behind the needs of others. Or, to put it another way, an individual's ambitions or personal goals are subordinated to the good of others.

Truly narcissistic people are far too indulged with their own needs to consider helping others. Or if they do help others, it's usually part of some manipulation to gain an advantage. With a blatant 'out-for-yourself'' attitude, it's only a matter of time before narcissistic individuals take their fall. Enduring success, in whatever field, is intimately linked to unmistakable commitments toward advancing the success of others. The notion that 'private interest is best served by public interest' underscores the fact that self-indulgent success is frowned upon and not tolerated in most circles. Only work on behalf of the greater good provides the justification for personal self-aggrandizement. In order to advance your own personal cause, it's necessary to direct your energies toward improving the position of others. Only then can the road to the top be cleared of all its narcissistic debris.

Today's culture is replete with images of cutthroat grandiosity, leaving many individuals falsely concluding that to make progress you must bulldoze others in your path. Misleading images of 'rising to the top' invoke pictures of corporate players stabbing each other in the back on their upward rise. While it's true that egocentric gamesmanship occurs, it's overt expression must be carefully masked with unselfish motives and actions. Conspicuous selfishness or callous disregard for others invites a host of retaliatory actions, and is clearly a prescription for failure.

Climbing to the top requires the help, whether we admit it or not, of many individuals whose own needs for support and assistance have to be taken into consideration. If you view the world as *your* service station, expecting others to serve only your interests, the climb up will indeed be treacherous. When you slip and need others' support, a helpful hand won't be outstretched when you need it most. Individuals prone toward selfishness and insensitivity find themselves short on friends and rely almost exclusively on themselves. "No man is an island," said the wise English statesman Benjamin Disraeli, attesting to the reality that *interdependency*--or relying on others' help and support--is the only formula for lasting success.

An ambitious, driven, but highly selfish young executive in the film industry managed to claw his way up the corporate ladder. Starting at the bottom and rising upward, many observed his pattern of engineering cosmetic relationships only to serve his needs. Once his power was secured, he'd abruptly usurp another person's position. Using fear and intimidation, he ruled by threats not by breeding any real loyalty or admiration. While interviewing for a new position, some of his grandiosity and self-serving personal philosophy leaked out. During the interview, he's asked what he can do for the company. Without hesitation, he indulges himself and confidently proclaims:

"Let's be up-front. The person currently in this position doesn't have a clue what he's doing. He's made one loser after another, going over-budget on most films and failing to read the pulse of the public. He's probably an OK 'creative type' but he doesn't understand 'the business.' You need someone in the position who can ride herd on these 'artists' and get the project made within budget. There's absolutely no excuse for this division running in the red."

After hearing a mouthful of his criticism [the interviewer was now wondering what Michael really thought of him], he decided to follow up:

"Michael, we already know why we're interviewing for this position. But we're still interested in finding out what you'd bring to the table. We're also aware of the fact that several of your recent projects have also flopped. None of us are psychic and all of us make mistakes but I didn't hear what you'd do differently. If I missed something, please fill me in."

Thrown off by the interviewer's comments, Michael tried to collect himself:

"Look, Jack. I'm a graduate of USC film school. I don't have to sit here and itemize my credentials. You know Jim [the one in the current position] is in over his head. As I told you, staying in-budget is a very important part of maintaining profit on these low-budget films."

Feeling inclined to respond, Jack took the liberty to say:

"Michael, everyone is well aware of your credentials. There's no question that you're more than qualified for the position. But with your highly critical way of presenting yourself, I have strong reservations about whether you can manage an insecure staff which needs constant hand holding."

You don't have to be a psychic to figure out whether Michael ever got the job. His arrogance, insensitivity, conceit and grandiosity sealed his fate. Regardless of his many credentials, his excessive criticality and inflated self-image made him a stressful enough job interview, not to mention a prospective management employee. Without showing some self-awareness and restraint over one's narcissistic propensities, persuading others to follow your lead is a tough road to hoe. It's unrealistic to expect fair evaluations from others when you've acted in a blatantly offensive manner. Although it's one thing to be vain, it's still another to allow your grandiosity to burden others. In a narcissistic world, selling yourself is a balancing act between presenting your best side and calculating your impact on your audience. For those seeking the magic of charisma and all it brings, controlling narcissistic tendencies is a top priority.

Putting a Lid On Grandiosity

Containing narcissistic propensities is a matter of survival not just preference. Displaying a superior attitude has no place in the lives of individuals seeking advancement in careers or elsewhere. The line between self-confidence and grandiosity is difficult for many people because they have trouble determining when they've crossed the acceptable limit. It's one thing to itemize your credentials, but it's still another to arrogantly proclaim your superiority. Grandiose displays assure that your charisma will almost certainly melt-down. Nothing turns people off more than unsightly grandiosity.

Many people find themselves wanting confidence but not knowing the difference between communicating their assets and selfishly trumpeting their talents. While it's OK for others--like agents, managers, publicists, relatives, friends, etc.--to boast about your abilities, it's not OK for you to do the same. Self-appraisals, by their very nature, tend to be somewhat inflated, and when you're sounding your own horn it doesn't show much class. Self-congratulatory comments are viewed as conspicuously self-serving, and do very little to advance your personal power. At the same time, it doesn't mean that when discussing your attributes you need to be your own worst critic.

A journeyman applicant for a chemical engineering position is being interviewed by a prospective employer. Although he received his training south of the border, he's considered highly competent and posts excellent experience. The employer is trying to make the best possible appraisal of whether his skill-level matches the requirements of the position sought. During the interview the employer asks:

"Mr. Bennett, as you may know, there are many well qualified candidates applying for this position. We consider you among the most experienced and best qualified. Would you kindly tell us, in your own words, why you believe you're best qualified for the job?"

Feeling somewhat reticent to blow his own horn, Mr. Bennett comments:

"As you can see on my resume, I received my engineering training at a private institute in Mexico. I went there because they were the only ones who would take a chance on someone from a nursing background. Before changing careers, I put myself through school doing vocational nursing. When I realized I was good in math, a counselor suggested I try engineering--and the rest is history. Yes, I've had many different types of engineering jobs and consider myself a good generalist. I may not be in the same class as my Ivy League 'friends' but I can hold my own."

After hearing Mr. Bennett's description, the interviewer asked a few more perfunctory questions and ended the interview. Just as excessive grandiosity risks offending your audience, maligning yourself is no help either. When low self-esteem troubles individuals, they have difficulty finding good things to say about themselves. Possessing high self-esteem, ironically, also doesn't result in self-grandiosity, arrogance, conceit or insensitivity. No, these are conspicuous symptoms of ego weakness: A kind of fragility which leads to erratic and self-defeating behavior. And certainly not the essential high-level intangibles needed to move up the ladder.

Narcissism or pathological selfishness is a defense against damaged or weakened self-esteem. Individuals with healthy self-esteem don't hoard their talents or flagellate others with their own insecurities. They graciously offer support to others with the expectation that they're rewarded with the internal satisfaction of knowing that they've improved someone's position. Individuals with low self-esteem experience someone else's success as a slap in the face. They find themselves comparing and competing with others and wind up on the short end of the stick. Besieged with petty emotions--like envy, jealousy and anger--the narcissist's relationships are frequently disturbed. Without normal bonding, they fail to develop the necessary social connections to advance themselves.

Recognizing how self-esteem impacts your grandiosity goes a long way in alerting you to how this counterproductive attitude interferes with success. Knowing that you have narcissistic propensities automatically alerts you that you have to compensate for this weakness. Spending time on the couch won't hurt, but is not wholly necessary. What's needed is (a) having the *awareness* that this stubborn bugaboo exists and (b) compensating by tuning-in to the needs of others. Some might ask: If it were really that easy, why wouldn't all narcissists make those changes? The answer is simple but not easy: Most narcissists aren't cognizant of the fact that (a) they're grandiose and arrogant and (b) that selfish behavior hurts their chances of success. When they figure this out, most rational people are willing to make the 'minor' sacrifices.

A selfish, self-serving businessman, whose major preoccupation was himself, fell in love with the women of his 'dreams.' His only problem was the fact that she saw through his selfishness and wanted nothing to do with him. She wouldn't even give him the time of day. You see, she'd had her heart broken once and vowed that she'd never be vulnerable again. Watching him strut around like the Marlboro man turned her off--big time. But his love for her

was so great that he would do anything. Recognizing that he
had to change his ways, he decided to take another tact:
Abandon his narcissism. He began showering her with
flowers, perfume and gifts. Finally his overtures paid off
and her resistance softened. In a phone conversation, he
shared some of his feelings:

"You know Sally . . . I'm the most selfish man in the
world. I admit it! For most of my life I've served only one
person--myself. But now that's all changed. The only thing
I want to do now is find special ways of making you happy.
I know you don't trust me. But over time you'll see that I
can't live without you. You're the most important thing in
my life--not myself anymore. Just wait, you'll see."

Although a bit extreme, what we've witnessed is the
recognition that narcissism or grandiosity would get Mr.
Jones nowhere. By changing his attitude from one of
extreme selfishness to unconditional giving, his life was
transformed and he got what he wanted. Without this
change, Sally never would have never trusted him to expose
her vulnerability. As it was, she eventually gave in to all his
selfless giving. By controlling his selfishness and casting
bread upon the water, he exceeded all expectations. Had he
remained fixated on his own needs, his relationship never
would have developed. How many situations do you know
in which less selfishness and more giving would pay-off
handsomely? No doubt many. By redirecting his energies
and tuning-in to someone else's needs, he was richly
rewarded. If you asked Mr. Jones what he thought his
chances were of landing this relationship, he would have
told you, "Slim and none!"

Empathy Pays Its Weight in Gold

Whatever ways narcissism damages charisma, empathy rehabilitates it by creating instant approachability and bonding. While grandiosity creates coldness and alienation, empathy generates warmth and connectedness. Empathy is one of the most powerful elements of charisma and the best antidote to grandiosity. It's an indispensable part of tact and diplomacy and dramatically increases persuasive power. Without empathy, your sphere of influence is markedly narrowed. And yet as valuable as this quality is to success, some people can't seem to buy it for any price. Those who are lucky enough to possess empathy have the leverage to orchestrate their agenda.

Showing genuine interest in others automatically establishes familiarity and closeness. Even where people come from disparate cultures or backgrounds, empathy provides the bridge to common experience. Tuning-in and paying undivided attention to another person's experience is the best way of establishing satisfying relationships. To this exact extent, empathy allows otherwise self-serving individuals to appear caring and considerate. After all, what creates more intimacy than listening attentively and hearing someone out? As easy as this seems, it might be the hardest thing you'll ever do. Most people find it far easier to talk than listen. Demonstrating the patience and sensitivity to truly listen to others is easier said than done. Combating the tendency to ventilate frustrations and use people as sounding boards requires considerable restraint. If accomplished, it really pays off.

A 40 year old physician and inveterate bachelor is having considerable difficulty finding the 'right' relationship. Exasperating his family for years, they've all but given up on seeing him married. Despite going on literally hundreds of dates, he always complains that he just hasn't met the right person. Finally, he feels excited about meeting an outstanding prospect. On their second date, he starts sharing a little more of himself:

"Susie, you won't believe how many patients I was forced to see today. It was non-stop! This HMO I'm working for is really trying to kill me. It seems like they're paging me all night long--I can't get any sleep. Just look, I never had bags under my eyes and now I look like a wreck. If I knew then, what I know now, I never would have gone into medicine. Why should I have to be a slave to an HMO. This is ridiculous. I used to like being a doctor, now I dread going to work."

After hearing this mouthful, Susie tried to change the subject and talk a little bit about herself. Trying to take Bill off the subject, she says:

"Yeah . . . I've been reading how hard it is for doctors now. But just look on the brighter side--it beats unemployment! Bob, did you see '*As Good As It Gets*?' Wasn't that a romantic movie. I just loved the way he finally opened up and showed his love to her. I notice you haven't commented about *my* dress OR my new earrings. Do you like them? How about the movie?"

Reacting to Susie's comments, Bill reluctantly says:

"Yeah, they're nice. Now, I have to figure out what I'm going to do with the office manager. She's the one responsible for filling up my schedule. I don't know how much longer I can take this schedule. I really don't know how to confront her. She's overloading me with patients. What do you think I should say to her?"

Noticing that Bob was minimally interested in her story and only wanted to talk about his problems, Susie began getting impatient. She remarked:

"Bob, grow up! You're making decent money, driving a new BMW, and contributing to your 401K. You've really got to stop whining about your situation at work. Just deal with it for Christ's sake. If your not happy, start looking elsewhere."

Without having a crystal ball, it appears that Bob will be continuing his interminable search for the 'right' mate. His oblivious insensitivity, grandiosity, sense of entitlement and inability to focus on anything other than his own problems, makes developing a lasting relationship untenable. As much as he says he wants a commitment, what he's really looking for is a sounding-board on which to relieve his anxieties. Although he appears good on paper and a 'nice guy,' he's actually self-absorbed to the point that he can't engage in mutually satisfying and reciprocal communication. His selfish monologue might provide some temporary relief, but it left him isolated, alone and withdrawn. Had he been able to show his date a modicum of empathy things might have turned out differently.

After a few weeks without a phone call from Susie, Bob began a little self-reflection. Although he only remembered fragments of her comments, he was left with the idea that he was too selfish and preoccupied. Realizing that conveying empathy could pay off, he decided to tune-in to her needs when and if they ever met again. Finally, she returned one of his calls. This time the conversation went differently. Armed with the insight that he must try to be less narcissistic and more empathic he says:

"Susie, please forgive me for seeming so self-centered on our last date. I'm sorry I get so upset about work. That's clearly not your problem. Anyway, I actually did notice your new dress and earrings. That dress looked great on you. And those earrings, they were so classy. You've got great taste! I only wish I had the flair for fashion that you do. Maybe we should go out again and you can help me put some outfits together. I think you've got a greet sense of style."

By tuning-in to Susie's needs and giving her undivided attention, Bob was automatically moving from the bench to scoring some serious points. Validating her sense of taste and refinement helped Bob clearly place his focus away from his own problems and onto the indispensable process of relating. His sensitive and empathic remarks were greatly appreciated and led to a strong attraction. As turned off as she was on the first date, she was equally turned-on with the second go-around. Clearly becoming more empathic and less narcissistic sparked the turn around. For those thinking that selfishness is the path to success, they should be reminded that it's actually a big turn-off. Since most people are inherently selfish and want their needs met, trying a healthy dose of empathy might be the shortest distance between satisfying others *and* getting your own needs fulfilled.

Apart from making directly validating remarks, empathy is best conveyed by improving your attention and listening skills. Monopolizing conversations might feel good temporarily, but it eventually backfires. Because most people crave opportunities to express themselves and relate their feelings, it only makes sense that spending more time listening--and less time talking--opens many doors. That's not to say it has to be a one-way street. Ironically, by training yourself to listen more, you'll have a far more receptive audience in which to be expressing your own personal business. Aside from dramatic expression and speaking, good listening skills are a helpful high-level intangible involved in creating charisma. As we've said, haughtiness, arrogance, grandiosity and self-obsession are your best assurance of sabotaging your personal power.

Stop Looking in the Mirror

Developing charisma involves more than staring at yourself in the mirror and telling yourself you're great. In fact, one of the downfalls of grandiose people is spending far too much time engaged in self-indulgent activities-- including looking in mirrors. While paying attention to your health and appearance is a prerequisite to lasting success, obsessional preoccupation with your looks and body wastes precious time which could be put to better use. For many fitness fanatics, it's more related to weight management and appearance, than to improving health or exercise tolerance. There's a blurry line between maintaining health and compulsive activities. Today's exercise mania, for many people, is less related to fitness and health and more related to cosmetics and vanity.

Narcissistic individuals spend so much time preening their cosmetic selves that they lose sight of the warning signs of 'religious' self-preoccupation. By remaining too self-absorbed, important opportunities are easily missed. How many traffic accidents do you think are caused by narcissistic inattention? Running into trees or fire hydrants while combing hair, inspecting age-lines or touching-up mascara is more common than you think. Narcissists must make a concerted effort to redirect their energies away from themselves and toward the outside world.

As long as someone is internally focused, it's difficult for them look clearly at crucial opportunities. Especially when dealing with people, many 'me-focused' people miscalculate the intentions and motivations of others. It's difficult to size-up or read people when everything you see is a carbon copy of your own needs or wants. How can you possibly deal with the needs of others when you're obsessed with yourself? It pays to remember that when you place yourself second, you'll usually come out on top.

A president of a publicly traded health care corporation is spending far more time grooming himself than managing the company store. Instead of reviewing earnings' reports and profit and loss statements, he's more easily found at his cosmetic surgeon's office, health club or shopping for Armani suits. Rather than meeting with his management team, he's posing for snap shots in the gym. While he's busy massaging his vanity, there's serious morale problems at the corporate headquarters. One of his main lieutenants apparently mutinied and denounced him to the board of directors. Tipping them off about his priorities, they're told he's more invested in his own fitness than the company's. At a recent board meeting, he's confronted by one of his directors:

"Brian, forgive me for having the unenviable task of giving you some feedback. We've been told that you spend more of your time working out than you do in meetings for the business. We all appreciate your commitment to fitness, but your staff seems frustrated with your priorities. What do you have to say for yourself?"

Looking stunned by the accusations, the president reacts defensively:

"Sam, how could anyone question my loyalty or service to the company? How can anyone expect me to develop this company as a lean, mean machine, if its president is obese and sedentary? Yes, I do try to keep myself fit. But suggesting that's all I do is preposterous! There's evidently a lot of jealous people scrutinizing my every move. I can't help the way I look. I'm not obsessed with myself as some would have you believe. I just happen to think that health and fitness are an important part of running a company."

Responding to Brian's defensive reaction, Sam takes another shot:

"Brian, I don't think you 'get it!' I'm not begrudging you a healthy lifestyle. I'm trying to give you some feedback that you've turned everyone off and are in your own little world. If you can't relate to your staff--regardless of your own appraisal--how can you manage this business? We're here today to report to you that we will not be picking up the option on your contract."

Grandiosity comes in many different forms and packages. Although you might be the nicest person in the world, if you're too self-absorbed you'll still be regarded as insensitive and oblivious. Whether you're indulging yourself with excessive vanity or various diversions--like drugs, alcohol, binge eating, compulsive gambling or even excessive sexuality--essential information will be missed. Brian's troubles stemmed from the fact that his mind was directed toward his own narcissistic interests rather than his work or his staff. Had he been less narcissistic, he would have made the needed adjustments to save his job. By the time he found out there were serious problems, it was already too late. As you can see, there's a murky line between self-love and self-abuse.

While we've noted the downside to grandiosity and self-absorption, the other side of the coin is also risky: Having a disregard for your personal fitness and health. Paying too little attention to one's appearance is also self-defeating. Bingeing on food, drugs and alcohol, sex or any other diversion which leads to deteriorated health also leads to a loss of charisma. Sometimes there's a reason for having mirrors: To receive accurate feedback about yourself. If you find yourself looking away too often, it might indicate that you're in denial about something you don't want to face. Having the courage--and the ego strength--to look honestly in the 'mirror' and accept constructive feedback goes a long way in helping direct you on the path to success. Ignoring the necessary cues about yourself, often leads to disappointment and failure.

A gifted, highly successful comedian has taken the entertainment industry by storm. His manic and outrageous humor has resulted in abundant TV and movie opportunities. Unfortunately, his mania wasn't limited to his acting career but extended to all facets of his life. Prone toward a life in the fast lane, his continuous binge on food, drugs, alcohol, sex and gambling have contributed to his agent's premature hair loss. Gaining nearly 100 pounds, suffering from chronic insomnia, hyping himself on drugs, smoking like a chimney and now diagnosed with high blood pressure, his agent tries to share his concerns. During a rare moment on a long flight to a movie location, he says:

"Jimmy, I'm really concerned for your health. For the past year, I've watched you gain nearly 100 pounds, fool around with countless women, binge on drugs and alcohol and go without sleep for days at a time. Now Dr. Kim has told you your blood pressure is dangerously high. By anyone's standards, you're on a collision course with a heart attack or stroke. I'm really scared! Why aren't you?"

Falling on deaf ears, the obnoxious comedian says:

"Mark, that's ridiculous! I think your getting hysterical. There's really no cause for alarm. OK, so my weight's up a little bit. Since when are you such a saint? Just last week we were doing 'lines' together. Now you're putting a guilt-trip on me? Really! It sounds like you're more concerned whether I'll be healthy enough to meet my contractual obligations--isn't that really it? Stop preaching so damn much--you sound like my mother."

Exasperated by the comedian's defensiveness, his agent remarks:

"Jimmy, just try--for once in your life--to hear me out. I'm not the only one who's concerned about you. I was the one given the unhappy task of trying to get through to you. It's not just me . . . everyone's concerned about your health. The fact that you're the least concerned is my biggest fear. Look . . . I feel it's my duty as a concerned friend to give you some feedback. Take it any way you wish. At least, when you keel over, I'll know I tried to get through to you. So do what you want with this. This is the last time I'm going to hassle you about these things. OK . . . just forget it!"

Sensing his concern but still in denial, Jimmy reacts:

"Mark, 'thanks for your concern' but, trust me, I've got it under control. What I don't need right now is extra pressure from my agent about my personal habits. I'm under enough stress from everyone else--including everyone who's constantly hitting me up for money. If I feel like doing something that relaxes me then that's a good thing. Right? Let's just drop it. How about it?"

When narcissism blinds individuals from seeing their own self-destructive behavior, getting through can be a piece of work. With this type of defect, it's hard to talk about developing high-level intangibles or anything else when the person is going down the tubes. As you can see, Jim's denial was so air-tight that he proceeded to rationalize his shortcut to suicide. In Jim's case, it was regrettably too late as he eventually died of a massive coronary, perhaps aided by a drug overdose.

Should narcissistic self-abuse threaten an individual's life, then it's advisable to get professional help. If that's not possible, the least we can do is to give the person some concerned but honest feedback. Whether the unsolicited advice is taken or not is of less consequence. The fact it's been offered in a concerned fashion leaves at least some chance--no matter how slim--of getting through. You've at least done your job and maybe saved a life.

Co-Dependency 'Some More'

Co-dependency, or the tendency toward excessive giving or self-sacrifice in relationships, suggests that orienting yourself around the needs of others is pathological. Can you imagine, with all the failures in relationships, only being out for yourself? How long would your relationship last if you were only concerned with meeting your own needs? Not too long! Judging by the escalating rate of divorce, the narcissistic--or me first--approach hasn't worked. Common sense tells anyone involved in lasting relationships that selfishness is a prescription for failure.

Sharing or reciprocation is alien to the narcissist's vocabulary. Since co-dependency is the opposite of narcissism, it only makes sense that individuals cured of co-dependency could wind up narcissistic. Funny, isn't it, how if you go too far in any direction, you end up in exactly the same place. Most relationships thrive on reciprocal co-dependency or two people each orienting themselves around the needs of their partner. What's wrong with this? When you think of it, without some type of mutual giving or self-sacrifice, relationships become a vehicle for exploiting people. Very few people can sustain a relationship in which their partner is always taking and never giving. It just won't work! So maybe co-dependency isn't such a bad thing after all.

Co-dependency is a far more predictable formula for success than narcissism for developing a host of cooperative relationships. Although it seems that narcissists are 'out for themselves,' the truth is that their selfishness fails to win them leverage with people. In today's social marketplace co-dependent people are viewed as pathological and narcissists are accepted as par for the course. It's almost expected that contemporary relationships are inherently narcissistic. Is it any wonder that relationship failures are occurring at alarming rates? Contrary to popular misconceptions about gender differences, relationship failure is caused more often by just plain selfishness.

Successful politicians are well aware of the fact that the best platform is catering to the needs of their constituents--not, as some would have you believe, their own. Addressing their own eccentric needs or those of a small but influential minority is also a prelude to disaster. The secret is actually quite simple: Look beyond yourself and find special ways of addressing the needs of others. Whether your audience is one or many, you still have to find and relate to someone else's pulse.

A presidential candidate, whose major campaign planks have included promoting constitutional amendments banning abortion and balancing the Federal budget, finds himself lagging in the polls. Attempting to jump-start his sagging campaign, his manager suggests he begin promoting more relevant issues like education. The candidate reluctantly decides to follow his advice--but only in his way. At a whistle-stop, he speaks to an enthusiastic crowd:

"We are here today to announce our new priority and plan for the future--education. For too long, we've accepted mediocrity in our public schools. We simply have to acknowledge the fact that today's public education system is a failure. It's been long recognized that the elite of this country send their children to private schools. Our plan involves making private education within the reach of every American. By offering tax incentives and vouchers, average Americans can finally give their children a chance of a good education. Why shouldn't the average American family be able to give its children the benefits of private education?"

By imposing his own needs on the education issue, the candidate sadly miscalculated the needs of his audience-- many of whom were public school teachers. Trashing their livelihood and promoting his own agenda that ignores the basic needs of his audience, sadly misses the mark--and evidently the electorate concurs. As we've said, tuning-in to your audience and addressing *their* needs promotes the kind of charisma necessary to advance your agenda.

Certainly saying and doing things which offends others and hurts your cause should be examined very carefully: Most people simply can't afford making costly mistakes. Obviously, there are many reasons why people who 'ought to know better' self-destruct, but there's little excuse for not developing some simple awareness of your impact on others. There are countless business and social situations in which expanded awareness and insight helps individuals orchestrate their agenda. Without awareness and insight--especially about considering the needs of your audience--achieving your goals is a wasteful uphill battle.

The athletic director of a prestigious university finds himself under the gun. Taking heat from the board of regents due to a precipitous drop in revenue, the university president has been put on notice that they'd better see some changes--sooner rather than later. With shrinking profit sharing from lucrative TV contracts, the president holds a private meeting with the athletic director [AD] to share his concerns. Without saying that his job is on the line, the president presses on with his message:

"Lenny, Coach Dunbar just isn't cutting it. Let's face it, we've outlived our reputation now and alumni support and TV revenue is dropping like a rock. As you know, his multi-year contract can't be afforded without the university receiving substantial profits from TV contracts. With our record, no one's interested in picking up TV rights to our games. Without some big changes, you and I both are going to be standing in the help wanted lines."

Sensing the threat, the athletic director, known for his bravado and assertiveness, reacts defensively and says:

"Look Frank, I'm not the one who ratified Coach Dunbar's contract--it was you and the board of regents. You're the one's that had to have Dunbar. I favored promoting the assistant coach. Remember? Yes, Dunbar's ultimately to blame--it's his show. But, let's face it, I've done everything to enhance this university's prestige. I'm not going to take the heat for something that I didn't do. You and the regents have to take some responsibility."

With his fuse getting short, the president reacts:

"Lenny, you don't get it!: 'Little bugs climb the backs of big bugs, and littler bugs climb the backs of little bugs, ad infinitum.' My job is on the line . . . and so is yours. If we don't turn this program around quickly--and I mean quickly--our jobs are history. I'm not interested in excuses or who's to blame, I'm interested in results. Now, you've got your orders, do something about it!"

Lenny's lack of charisma in handling the crisis reflects directly on his poorly developed high level-intangibles of tact and diplomacy. Reacting to the president's obvious stress, he would have been far better off responding to his needs. As it was, his need to defend himself and blame others for the program's failure, only antagonized an already tense situation. Once again, rather than self-assertion, less narcissism and more healthy co-dependency might have conveyed a different message to the president. It's not *Phi Beta Kappa* to discount or trivialize some one else's concerns. That only leads to more antagonism and defensiveness. Had the athletic director shown more charisma and remarked:

- "I totally understand what you're saying," or

- "I don't blame you for feeling the way you do," or

- "Your have every right to be concerned," or even better,

- "Let's come up with a way of fixing the problem," etc., he might have bought himself some precious time in which to enlist the president's support. It's not charismatic to repudiate others in positions of authority or power: It's self-destructive! Controlling your initial impulses and calculating responses which defuse a tense situation, doesn't come naturally for most people. By looking beyond your own needs--whether it's defending yourself or lashing out-- and figuring out what you could do or say to improve someone else's position, your charisma will be shifted into a higher gear.

Arrogance, Ignorance and Stupidity

Charismatic people don't allow their egos to prevent them from learning new and valuable information: They certainly don't permit their personalities to self-destruct. Narcissists, on the other hand, are know-it-alls whose bravado and arrogance prevents them from acknowledging the fact that they have a lot to learn. Always portraying a phony grandiose self to the public, narcissistic individuals have great difficulty admitting any weakness or inferiority. Much of their energy is invested in blowing smoke or defending this pretentious image of brilliance and power. Challenging them often shatters their confidence and self-esteem, sometimes resulting in angry outbursts or temper tantrums-- also known as 'narcissistic rage.' Like most infantile reactions, it passes quickly and doesn't carry much weight.

Because of this ego-weakness, narcissists are highly defensive, almost paranoid, frequently misinterpreting innocent social interactions as put-downs or denunciations. Barricading themselves in their own protective world or limiting their associations to a coterie of sycophants and individuals whose inferiority in various areas is known by all, they're not receptive to 'real' relationships. Only then do narcissists feel adequate. Believing that the adulation is real or commensurate with their actual abilities, narcissists develop inflated self-esteem which is quickly shattered by ordinary disappointments, easily endured by individuals with 'normal' self-worth. With their phony grandiose self, narcissists become 'legends in their own minds.'

Although narcissists appear haughty and grandiose, their emotional vulnerability leaves them avoiding unpredictable and challenging situations in which their abilities are truly tested. While charismatic people are inquisitive and seek out feedback from which to refine their skills, narcissists avoid objective feedback, fearing criticism and ultimately ego-deflation. It's this defensive posture in which they avoid real contact with people, which leaves them impervious to learning new and better ways of acting.

Relying on old skills and information, narcissists often fail at rather routine tasks. Without the ability to process useful feedback, they're prone toward making repetitive mistakes. Unable to learn from experience, narcissists are hopelessly trapped in a vicious cycle rendering them incapable of learning. Guess what, if you can't profit from experience, you're going to make potentially irreversible mistakes. Everyone makes mistakes, but it's the speed with which you make needed corrections--not the fact that you made mistakes--which determines whether you'll wind up successful.

Displaying a defensive arrogance leaves narcissists impervious to learning new and improved ways of making important adjustments. Without processing new information, it's difficult to profit from experience and you end up making the same mistakes, when you should have known better. Charismatic individuals are constantly reevaluating themselves and learning everything they can to advance their position. While interacting with people, they know how to ingratiate themselves just enough to gain a strategic advantage. On the contrary, narcissists are too busy guarding their fragile egos to soak-up the necessary information to achieve their goals.

A nationally known network sports announcer, whose personal relationships were contributing to his agent's painful gastrointestinal distress, is engaged in a sado-masochistic relationship with his long-time girl friend. He's been urged by his agent and personal attorney to control his proclivities toward reckless sexual behavior. Believing that he's immune to adverse publicity, his agent warns him about the morals' clause in his contract. On a flight back to Manhattan, after a near-miss collision with the paparazzi at an undisclosed motel, his agent confronts him and says:

"Mel, what the hell are you doing? Do you have any clue what it's taken for us to get to this point in your career? You're playing Russian roulette--and for what? My goodness man . . . get a grip on yourself! You're flirting with disaster. How do you think the network would take an allegation of moral depravity? Not too well. Look, I know you think your their superstar, but don't push your luck. I've told you how vindictive your 'friend' is--what's it going to take to wake you up?"

Not really 'getting it' but responding flippantly to his agent's concerns, Mel says:

"Look Jack, I know you're under stress, but I think it might help for you to visit Dr. Goldberg when you return to Manhattan. He's got some great 'scripts' to help control your anxieties. Really, it's out-of-hand. Give me a little credit . . . I've been at this game for some time. Believe me, they [corporate executives] love me at the network. They wouldn't dare screw with my contract--their ratings would drop like a rock. It's all about ratings and advertising revenue. And I know for a fact that I'm their sponsors' favorite. Jack, you really need to chill!"

After 'hearing Mel out,' Jack's stress level really was on its way over the top. Reacting to Mel's oblivious remarks, his agent still feels compelled to comment:

"Mel, I'll agree with you on one thing: I *am* under stress. But it's because of your reckless behavior. You're not just playing a dangerous game of brinkmanship with *your* life-- but you're also screwing with mine. I can't believe you're that selfish. Flirting with disaster might turn you on, but I think it's nuts. Do you expect me to sit back and watch you toss your career into the wastebasket? I don't think so. If you've decided to self-destruct, why should I be dragged down with you? You think you're indispensable--don't you? Your ego is really out of control! No one is irreplaceable--not even you. Get a grip!"

Reeling from Jack's attack, Mel's fuse begins to blow. He reacts [with arrogant grandiosity] and says:

"Jack . . . you're out of line. It's low-life's like you who've been screwing me for years. You guys are all alike. You're nothing without me. Your problem is that you start thinking that you're the one whose got the talent. How dare you question my judgment? In case you're wondering-- you're fired!"

Bereft of real self-worth and charisma, narcissists' fragile exterior are easily punctured by anyone daring to challenge their judgment or authority. Mel's defensiveness leaves him seismographically sensitive to criticism and prone toward rages. His childish grandiosity is unmistakable. Like an over-inflated balloon, he's easily deflated and inclined toward lashing-out. Unable to take criticism, narcissists insulate themselves from receiving constructive feedback and remain painfully ignorant. Without digesting new information, they continue to make the same old mistakes.

Managing narcissists is indeed challenging to their handlers, especially when they get themselves into hot water and need constant damage control. For their many handlers and significant others, it's unfortunately a rollercoaster ride filled with frenetic ups and downs and spectacular successes and failures: Like the 4th of July, the fireworks fizzle all too quickly.

Arrogance [the defense against depression and low self-esteem], *ignorance* [the inability to process new information] and *stupidity* [the inability to profit from experience], make developing lasting charisma a tough order to fill. By alerting narcissistic individuals to these propensities, it's possible to help them get a handle on their predictable path to self-destruction. Although they'll resist with all their might, by patiently showing concern and support and stroking them in special ways, they'll be open--ever more slightly--to constructive feedback. Dealing with narcissists is a delicate ballet in which tact and diplomacy are your best friends. Attempting to confront them directly rarely yields anything other than rebelliousness and hostility.

The president and CEO of a large publicly traded corporation in the grocery industry, known for his short fuse and explosive outbursts, is meeting with his senior managers at an annual corporate retreat. Having built the company from scratch, he often takes liberties not taken by many people. Standing at the lectern, addressing the group over lunch about competitive forces in the marketplace, he unveils a poster in which he facetiously outlines his personal philosophy. It reads:

"WE'LL GET ALONG JUST FINE AS LONG AS YOU
RECOGNIZE THE FACT THAT I'M GOD."

Although some chuckles are audibly heard, his senior
managers are really disgusted with his arrogance, conceit
and grandiosity. Feeling intimidated but wanting to address
some real issues, one of his regional managers says:

"Mr. Klein, our customers are telling us that we're now
priced about 10% above the competition. Although they
recognize our name and quality, it's becoming a more
difficult sale. Isn't it time to adjust prices downward to
match the competition? In our territory, we're losing market
share--and it's really a price issue."

Reacting defensively to his manager's comments, Mr.
Klein quips:

"Beasly, we're not in business to lose money or, for that
matter, to price match with every fly-by-night competitor.
Just remember where your pay raises come from. Why do
you feel at liberty to cut revenue to the company, but
unwilling to take a commensurate pay cut to your salary?
I've built this company by driving prices up not down. It's
just bad medicine to lower prices to compete with cheap
foreign imports. Let's stop being negative. We need to
increase our profit margins!"

Reeling from his stinging rebuff, Beasly composes himself
and takes a different tact with his obdurate boss. He says:

"Mr. Klein, you've created the most envied and prestigious
grocery business in this region of the country. No one
delivers better quality produce and products than we do.
Your concept of giving incomparable personal service has

distinguished us from our competition. Raising prices is absolutely our goal. You're quite right about that. That's certainly our long-range plan. Right now, we need a strategy to eliminate our competition. The best way to do that is by giving retailers absolutely no reason for buying from them. Believe me . . . we're not off by very much. With a negligible price adjustment, I'm absolutely convinced we can put some of our competition out of business and expand our market share."

Reacting less defensively, the otherwise onerous Mr. Klein sounds a different tune and says:

"Beasly, now you're making sense! I had no idea you were such a smart player. It sounds to me like you've got a real plan. Whatever you need to do is OK by me. You just go for it."

As easy as it is to transform narcissists into a rage, it's just as easy to placate them and encourage their compliance. Let's face it, it pays to know your audience. If challenging narcissists gets you nowhere, then temporarily feeding their grandiosity makes good sense. It's really that easy! Just recognize the fact that 'you attract a lot more bees with honey than with vinegar,' especially fragile individuals whose egos need constant massaging.

By learning to validate their narcissism, you've made a strategic step toward advancing your agenda and improving your charismatic skills. In Beasly's case, he wasn't in a position to confront his boss either about his unappealing personality or his questionable business savvy. But he's capable of plotting out a methodical strategy using timing, tact, diplomacy and by placating his boss. Only then, with careful calculation and planning, can you expect to orchestrate your agenda.

Taking a tactful, non-confrontational approach preempted the boss from targeting his employee for further criticism and attacks. While executing high-level intangibles requires added restraint, it pays rich dividends by reducing negativity and allowing both parties to claim victory. Giving someone the impression that they've gotten the better end of a deal shows maturity and self-control. If you're still soliciting approval and busy racking up points, you won't be able to stay in control of your situation. By controlling narcissistic propensities and orienting yourself around serving the needs of others, you'll be a quantum leap closer to reaching your goals.

Embracing Altruism

Although controlling narcissistic tendencies is a beginning first step in developing charisma, it's not enough to develop personal power. For this to occur, individuals must truly move from an attitude of self-centeredness to one oriented around the needs of others. As long as you're preoccupied with yourself and your own needs, you won't develop the charisma required to influence others. While grabbing everything for yourself seems productive, it's actually the surest way to wind up with nothing. Selfishness must be carefully disguised before it's considered acceptable. Conspicuously greedy individuals are eventually ostracized and find themselves low on the food chain of success and opportunity.

Altruism--or the unselfish interest in the welfare of others-- opens the door for many unexpected opportunities. Narcissism, on the other hand, invites a host of retaliatory gestures leading to personal and business failure. When you're perceived as selfish or egocentric, opportunities don't come knocking. Egregious selfishness--or an out-for-yourself attitude--is rarely tolerated even among those with unlimited resources and power.

Even eccentric tycoons whose wealth, power and resources seem limitless, can't afford to alienate people by displaying conspicuous selfishness. Flaunting wealth or power promotes envy, invites retaliation and is viewed as offensive. Despite their considerable resources, they need to carefully disguise greed and selfishness. No one wants to be around conspicuously selfish individuals. Selfishness is only tolerated when it's performed in the service of others. Or, to put it another way, unselfish-selfishness in which you're doing for others in order to help yourself, is very different from blinding greed or selfish-selfishness. Greed is considered OK as long as it's camouflaged by helping others.

Focusing your energy on serving the needs of others is the best assurance that your own needs will be met. When a politician talks about meeting the needs of his constituents he knows he's more likely to get reelected. If he's oriented toward his own agenda and lining his own pockets, he knows that his selfish motives, e.g., power, money, influence, status, etc., won't be realized. When you think about it, adopting an altruistic attitude is actually the most selfish thing that you can possibly do because it truly enables you to get your wishes filled. Remaining conspicuously selfish is the best guarantee that you'll wind up getting the short end of the stick.

An elected official has been arrested for alcohol intoxication and cocaine possession. He's admitted to using cocaine on the job, leaving many of his colleagues and the mayor infuriated and calling for his resignation. Because he's agreed to a court-ordered diversion program, his felony count won't be entered and the board can't evict him from his elected office. At a news conference he takes questions from the press. A reporter asks:

"Mr. Gonzalez, the public and your city board of governors have called for your resignation. How can you in good conscience continue to serve in your present position? Why is it OK to exclude applicants for civil service for past use but it's not OK to terminate city employees--like yourself-- for current drug use? Isn't it time for you to graciously step aside?"

Responding to the reporter's questions, the beleaguered city official remarks:

"Ms. Michaels, I'd be happy to respond to your questions. First of all let me just say I deeply regret hurting any of my colleagues and my constituents. I'm going to work hard toward once again earning their trust. I don't blame anyone for feeling betrayed and not trusting me. But my sobriety is my biggest priority so I can continue serving my constituency. No one has ever fought harder for their needs than I have. I feel it would be irresponsible to abandon them simply because I've been diagnosed with a treatable medical problem. Everyone's entitled to get some help for a real problem--and so am I."

Not satisfied with his response, the reporter takes another swipe and says:

"Mr. Gonzalez, how can you possibly justify staying in office? Even the mayor has called for your resignation. Isn't it time for you to step aside?"

Eager to respond, Gonzalez remarks:

"Ms. Michaels, once again, I don't blame you or anyone else for expecting me to step aside. I made a commitment to the people who put me here. Because I've had a problem doesn't mean I'm going to abandon my constituents. Since getting here, I've fought for the needs of my district and that's what I'm going to continue doing."

Although the politician is in deep water, his altruistic statements make his position less assailable. His expressed commitment toward serving the needs of his constituents clearly places their needs above his. By continuing to focus on his service to the public, his position is more secure. Avoiding defensiveness and rancor, also makes his position more stable. Had he lashed-out against the reporter, he would have further jeopardized his position by inviting retaliation through more relentless interrogation. Remaining affable and contrite, he's helped defuse the situation and improved his chances of political survival. By demonstrating altruism and restating his unequivocal commitment toward serving the needs of his district, he's helped his cause not--shot himself in the foot.

Can you imagine the public outcry had he said:

"I can't resign my position--I have no other means of supporting myself or my family. I have no savings and need my county paycheck. Besides which, alcohol and drug abuse are legitimate diseases . . . and I'm entitled to medical treatment. So what if I used cocaine on the job, so do thousands of other addicted Americans. Believe me, if I were able to retire, I'd gladly step aside. But I just can't afford to give up my job!"

Blatantly selfish, self-serving statements would be unacceptable and lead to more controversy. By couching things in altruistic gestures, Mr. Gonzalez has bought himself some more time. Since all controversy eventually loses heat, waiting it out is his best strategy for survival. Showing purely altruistic motives--no matter how feigned or insincere--goes a long way in preserving an otherwise untenable situation. Because the politician needs *his* paycheck, we can easily see how altruism was his best friend for survival. Again, 'private interest is always best served by public interest.'

A gubernatorial candidate, whose wealth and drive for political power were as salient as a red miniskirt, financed one of the costliest campaigns in the state's history. Without name recognition and with money to burn, he spent extravagant sums of his own personal fortune on TV advertising. Attempting to become a household word, his early TV ads focused on his philosophy and positions on key issues. As the election neared and his pollster reported that his numbers began slipping, his ads turned decidedly negative, preferring instead to attack his opponents on anything and everything. During a recent interview, he's questioned by a reporter about his tactics. The reporter asks:

"Mr. Minelli, how can you possibly justify spending your own personal fortune to subsidize your campaign? As you know, your opponents have solicited contributions from various groups and individuals. Public records indicate that you've received virtually no support from outside contributors. What does that say about your campaign?"

Showing considerable bravado, the candidate quips back:

"Mr. Jones, I'm not going to apologize for being rich. I don't need the contributions from outside individuals, groups or organizations. I'm the only candidate in this election not beholden to special interest groups. And that's a positive thing--not a negative. The fact that I've had to use my personal wealth should be seen as a blessing to voters."

Responding to Mr. Minelli's remarks, the reporter remarks:

"Mr. Minelli, we're all well aware of your personal wealth. But how can voters trust your agenda when you're the CEO of a major corporation. What are voters supposed to think when you have virtually no political track record and have failed to vote in the last 3 elections?"

With his fuse beginning to burn, the candidate reacts:

"Look . . . I don't need to be in politics to line *my* pockets. I'm the CEO of a publicly traded corporation. I don't see any conflict of interest whatsoever over the fact I'm a major share holder in a public corporation. As far as my past voting record, I think the candidates and the issues over the last few elections have been so boring that I couldn't bring myself to vote."

Grandiose, arrogant and insensitive statements like these do very little to stem controversy--in fact, they exacerbate it. Flaunting personal wealth or power has unappealing--even offensive--connotations to most people.   Ambitions for personal power and wealth should be carefully disguised and couched in altruistic motives. By exhibiting an inflated sense of self-importance and entitlement, the otherwise articulate candidate was made to look most unappealing.

Showing humility and remaining down to earth is the best formula for success. Although most people recognize that wealth and politics go together like ham and eggs, they still don't want someone's status and prestige thrown in their faces. If the candidate were to present himself in more altruistic terms, he'd have a lot better chance of attracting friends and winning votes.   As we've said, displaying narcissism strips-off your charisma and assures that success is one long step away.

Some Final Thoughts

Charisma is the priceless but fragile commodity responsible for personal power. It involves executing many high-level intangibles, including, tact, timing, diplomacy, common sense, high energy, awareness, etc., and is best expressed without appearing too self-centered. Grandiosity, self-obsession, arrogance, excessive vanity, and conceit have no place in the lives of charismatic individuals. Although some vanity or healthy narcissism are important for displaying charisma, conspicuous selfishness serves only one need: The self-defeating wish to fail, no matter what the venue.

Grandiosity and superiority are unwelcome traits for individuals seeking to build relationships and advance their careers. Although it's good to have self-confidence, it's a far cry from beating your chest and demanding unconditional approval and recognition. When your own neediness for validation eclipses your ability to show interest in others, it's difficult to develop any measure of influence over people. They tire quickly of individuals perceived as 'out-for-themselves.' While it's amusing for a limited time to be around colorful, self-centered people, it doesn't last long. They become boring very soon especially when their demandingness begins to outweigh your patience.

Developing charisma is intimately related to finding special ways to recognize and validate people. If you're preoccupied with soliciting your own recognition and approval, it's going to be difficult to extend yourself to others. As long as you're mired in your own neediness, developing charisma won't happen easily. It takes cracking out of your own shell and orienting yourself around fulfilling the needs of others, that builds charisma. By developing altruism--or unselfish interest in the welfare of others--and giving selflessly, you begin to see an unmistakable return on your investment.

Contrary to popular misconceptions, grabbing everything in your path has an uncanny way of boomeranging and is no assurance of success. In fact, acting pigishly invites unwanted notoriety and does very little to advance your cause. It's no accident--as we've said--that 'private interest is best served by public interest.' What this means is that orienting yourself around serving the interests of others pays the highest personal rewards. From this perspective, it only makes sense to be less egocentric and selfish and more oriented toward others. Although this seems paradoxical, it really works.

There's no disgrace in showing healthy co-dependency. The pendulum has clearly swung in the direction of retaining more co-dependent characteristics, especially where they involve ministering to the needs of others. As we've said, people tire easily of those consumed with themselves and relish the chance to remain involved with altruistic types. On the other side of the coin, knowing when to say when, or when to put your foot down and take care of yourself, is also important. You can't develop healthy charisma if you're so burned out giving to others that you've neglected yourself. Healthy co-dependency requires you to take care of your basic needs first before extending yourself to others. This goes without saying!

Developing powerful charisma is closely tied to controlling narcissistic propensities. While it seems like selfishness is the formula for success, it's actually a misleading mirage leading to rejection and failure. Showing empathy, expressing approval, and giving healthy doses of validation, assures that you'll have a more receptive audience to your overtures. Just as certainly, displaying grandiosity, arrogance and selfishness guarantees that it won't be long before you're looking at people's backs. Despite its counterproductive effects, narcissism still reigns supreme in many circles: It's a nasty habit which doesn't die easily. For those chasing the magic of charisma, it's a bad habit which must be given up.

Points to Remember

- Control grandiosity whenever possible

- Avoid displaying arrogance, conceit and superiority

- Remain approachable and down-to-earth at all times

- Show unconditional respect to your subordinates

- Display empathy when interacting with others

- Welcome honest feedback--no matter how unsettlingabout yourself

- Avoid excessive vanity and self-preoccupation

- Orient yourself toward meeting the needs of others

- Control defensiveness and remain open to new suggestions

- Adopt altruism as your personal philosophy for success

Chapter 3

IT'S ALL
ABOUT RELATING

In this chapter you'll learn about essential features of effective relating and developing charisma. • Introduction • Communication goes both ways • Energy's in short supply • Words do matter • Validation is the magic key • Humor's a great defense • Altruism is king • Implacable faith in human potential • Some final thoughts • Points to remember

Introduction

Relating involves more than simple communication: It's about establishing a 'meaningful' linkage or bond with another person. And without effective relating, developing charisma--or other interpersonal skills--is like playing Lotto: Winning is highly unlikely. We all know people who have OK communication skills but, for whatever reason, just can't relate. They seem trapped in a kind of self-absorbed bubble and have trouble creating satisfying relationships with anybody other than themselves. Yes, in case you're wondering, they're suffering from that old nemesis--narcissism.

Although they make perfunctory or even sincere attempts at communicating, it's almost like they're caught in a series of filters preventing them from getting through to others. Unable to transcend their own self-preoccupation, relating isn't in their vocabulary. While many people afflicted with this problem are genuinely motivated to communicate, they find themselves behind a brick wall.

Despite having reasonably good communication skills, they just can't bond on anything other than a superficial basis. They're able to talk about the weather, a restaurant, a movie, a newsworthy event, and especially about themselves, but completing a meaningful dialogue with another person is a different story. Talking more and more about less and less is symptomatic of this defective communication style. Quantity doesn't equal quality and beating your gums is no assurance that you'll get your point across. In fact, when verbal communication becomes excessive it creates intolerable noise in your audience--and you can readily expect a communication breakdown.

Incessant chatter practically guarantees that your efforts will fall on deaf ears. Spinning your wheels with a profusion of verbiage short-circuits most efforts at effective communication--except perhaps expressing pent-up frustration. Communication is just one small but important part of the relating process. Relating involves executing many *high-level intangibles*, e.g., tact, timing, consideration, diplomacy, awareness, good judgment, and, yes, common sense--all of which supersede other basic communication skills. Expressing articulate and precise language also doesn't guarantee relating. Nor do any other communication gimmicks like 'making appointments,' 'forced listening' or recognizing obvious 'gender differences.'

It's entirely possible to have excellent communication skills and wind up failing to relate. Relating--like other elements of charisma--is more correlated with *how* not *what* you communicate: Your appearance, emotional receptivity, style of delivery, timing, tact, awareness, good judgment and common sense all influence the relating process. Communication, on the other hand, is more associated with the message that you're trying to send. Any computer--or computer nerd--is capable of basic communication skills but may lack the *high-level intangibles* to actually relate to people.

Communication--not relating--is a process by which information is transmitted from a sender to a receiver. It involves many technical features, including, the content of the message, the characteristics of the sender and receiver, the style of delivery or reception, the context or situation, the history behind the communication or any other aspect occurring during the transmission. At any point in the communication process distortions and interference can occur resulting in failed communication.

A CEO of a large newspaper chain is addressing, for the first time, a group of employees at his most recent acquisition--an old established publication. Although he's been told that many of the employees are insecure about their jobs, he continues to relate his philosophy of corporate management. Addressing some of their concerns but following his own agenda, he says:

"First of all let me just say we're delighted to acquire this publication. We believe it has great promise for our corporation. What we try to achieve is 'economy of scale' and improved efficiency in the operation. In the coming weeks and months many of you will witness changes. You may be working longer hours and making less money, but we're committed to keeping the paper alive. Before taking the paper over, we were well aware of the paper's financial ills. We're going to do whatever is necessary to make this paper profitable again. Now, if you have any concerns, I'd be happy to take any of them."

Although there's a deafening silence in the audience, one of the senior writers dares to respond:

"Mr. Brenner, I've been working for the paper for the past 25 years. The management philosophy has always been oriented around quality reporting. They've rewarded us with some of the highest salaries in the industry. What do you intend to do?"

Feeling inclined to comment, the CEO says:

"We're absolutely committed to quality journalism. We expect that--like yourself--and wouldn't tolerate anything else. From our corporate perspective, you must try to understand how you're getting paid. If the current trends continue, we won't be talking raises, we'll be talking about bankruptcy and shutting the doors."

Apart from the fiscal realities of mergers and acquisitions, the CEO displays callous insensitivity to the legitimate insecurities of his recently inherited staff. His remarks lack charisma and mirror his own narcissistic agenda. Rather than address their insecurities, he adds to their fears by raising the specter of pay-cuts and layoffs. Although he must deal with certain realities, his comments--regardless of how true or factual--are bereft of tact, diplomacy and consideration. Instead of dealing with the employees' concerns, he imposes his own agenda. For a first meeting, he hasn't won too many friends. Once again, for comments to show charisma they must address the needs of others. A more savvy CEO, armed now with some *high-level intangibles*, might have related differently and said:

"Thank you for all joining us. We're delighted to have acquired your fine newspaper. And we're also well aware of your dedication and commitment to your jobs. We also know that this is a difficult time for everyone. Change doesn't come easily. But we're here to support your careers and do whatever it takes to make this transition smooth and effective. Although we'll all have to work hard to turn the paper around, working together there's nothing we can't do!"

Beating people over the head with the 'realities' of their situation does very little to reassure and comfort. Although most people want the facts, they also need support and reassurance. By utilizing the high-level intangibles of tact, diplomacy, sensitivity, positive energy, etc., the CEO cushions the blow of the paper's takeover and repercussions from the likely 'restructuring' coming down the pike. Because 'downsizing' creates risks of erratic behavior or even litigation, showing charisma isn't just a matter of preference--it's one of survival. When facing difficult circumstances, acting without charisma is your best guarantee that you'll increase your exposure and end up in hot water.

Communication Goes Both Ways

Communication is the process of sending and receiving messages; while relating is the job of bonding or connecting with people. If you're consumed with your own issues-- whether it's due to personal or physical problems or narrowed interests--it's difficult to make meaningful connections. It's one thing to have your own agenda, it's still another to ignore or disregard the special interests of others. By definition, conversation is a bilateral event. But, as you can imagine, it's difficult to keep score on who's playing the talker or listener. Because charisma is intimately involved in tuning-in to the needs of others, if you're too narcissistic you'll have considerable difficulty learning the art of reciprocation.

Actually, most conversations don't have to be perfectly balanced or reciprocal. While monopolizing conversations has its risks, each party in a meaningful dialogue doesn't require exactly equal time spent communicating. Egalitarianism has it place, but it's not the essence of relating or communication. Imbalances frequently exist in mutually satisfactory relationships. This should come as no big surprise. But when problems occur, it's usually because either one of the parties is dissatisfied or frustrated in the transaction. In other words, someone's needs aren't being met. And, as you can guess, it's entirely subjective and not based on some theoretical formula which counts syllables or the talk-time in a given conversation.

Charismatic people instinctively know when it's time to talk and when it's time to listen. Rather than imposing themselves, they show the sensitivity and awareness to know what works regardless of the situation. When it's said that 'communication is a two-way street,' it simply means you're showing some awareness of the other person's needs. In some conversations, you might do all the talking, because that makes the other person feel comfortable. In yet other circumstances, your role is one of disciplined and patient listening. How strange it is for some people to realize that some of the best 'conversationalists' say very little and listen abundantly. For people groping for things to say, it's a relief to know that they don't have to say anything!

Good conversationalists know it's not what you say but *how* you say it. Because most people are centered on themselves, they're not really that interested in what other people say. Although they do their best to look interested, they're only really concerned with their own agenda. This isn't a bad thing. It's just the reality of most conversations. Knowing this, it pays to show undivided attention when engaging in conversation.

Looking too disinterested or shifting your attention away from the dialogue, risks offending your audience, no matter how large or small. Attention, not the content of the message, creates the tone in conversations. Without undivided attention, the risks of alienating the second party in any communication is significantly higher. In case you're wondering, paying undivided attention doesn't necessarily involve talking: In most instances, it's about listening without interrupting.

An ambitious but overly zealous sales rep is having difficulty closing deals with various buyers. She doesn't have a clue what she's doing wrong. At sales meetings, she's an incessant talker, often monopolizing conversations to a point that she's dreaded by many buyers. Believing that everything she says is fascinating, she likes impressing people with endless anecdotal descriptions. At a recent sales presentation, the beat goes on and she's found saying:

"Margaret, so good to see you. I just got back from this fabulous cruise. I've got to tell you about it. You should have seen the buffets--they were incredible! Can you imagine, every kind of seafood under the sun: The shrimp, the lobster, the crab . . . Oh my God, it was unbelievable! You should have seen the desserts. They were amazing. Pastries, cakes, cookies . . . everything imaginable. Wow! You've got to go. Oh . . . did I tell you about the late-night snacks? The taco bar, the sandwiches, the dips, the drinks . . . It was phenomenal!"

Finding her eyelids getting heavy, the buyer had just about enough and remarks:

"Judy, are you aware of the fact that I've just lost 35 pounds on 'Weight-Watchers?' Why in God's name would I be interested in paying someone to go on a week-long binge? That'd be crazy! I thought you were here to show me those samples of the stainless steel, coffee travel mugs?"

Taken aback by the buyer's lack of interest, Judy comments:

"Margaret, you look great! I did notice something was different about you. But let me tell you: They also had the most unbelievable exercise equipment and aerobic classes on the boat. Although I never found my way to the gym, there's something in it for everyone. You would've had an incredible time!"

Showing self-defeating insensitivity, Judy is consumed with her own issues. Rather than tuning-in to Margaret's interests or needs, she continues to elaborate on areas clearly boring and even offensive to the very person she's seeking to influence. Her narcissism blinds her from seeing what's appropriate to discuss. Instead, regardless of how it's hurt her cause, she continues to impose her own agenda. The fact that she's 'into' eating doesn't mean that it's interesting to anyone other than herself. In effect, she's engaged in a monologue or parallel conversation. Had she remembered that Margaret was dieting, she might have talked about the jewelry or handbags she found at the ship's duty free shop. Instead, she allowed her own indulgence to dominate the conversation. For Judy, conversations weren't a two-way street.

Although no conversation--or relationship for that matter-- is truly bilateral, it doesn't mean you're at liberty to indulge yourself in your own whims. Talking too much about

yourself carries certain risks of miscuing your audience--
namely, you don't pick-up important feedback to change
directions or the subject. Successful conversationalists
know when it's time to stop talking and listen attentively.
While it's tempting to think that silence is golden, listening
isn't a passive process. It's not enough to simply let
someone else do the talking. Your eyes must not be
wandering from the ceiling to the floor or from the door to
the window.

It takes energy to show unwavering attention in
conversations. Even without uttering a word, it's still work
to concentrate on what someone's saying. *Eye contact* is an
integral part of showing intense focused attention.
Maximizing your charisma requires that eye contact should
neither be excessive nor inadequate. You can't realistically
show adequate attention when you're incapable of
maintaining good eye contact. Poor eye contact creates the
impression that your disinterested, bored, distracted or even
depressed. Certainly an unwanted message when you're
trying to develop your charismatic skills. Actually the two
[charisma and *poor* eye contact] are most incompatible.

Underlying poor eye contact are sometimes feelings of
inferiority, low self-esteem and possible fear or anxiety.
Should this be the case, you'll have to deal with it
professionally or otherwise. In many instances, poor eye
contact is just a matter of not paying good attention.
Sometimes just reminding yourself that it's an essential part
of demonstrating charisma automatically helps improve it.
On the other hand, excessive eye contact--or staring people
down--creates discomfort and should be avoided.
Attempting, like Svengali, to 'mesmerize' your audience
with excessive eye contact only breeds distress and erodes
charisma.

Eye contact is best utilized to control your audience's focus of attention. Without eye contact, attention is no longer focused and drifts from place to place. Let's face it, if you can't control attention in most business or social situations, you're not going to make the sale or orchestrate your agenda. Without maintaining undivided attention, making a solid interpersonal bond is going to be difficult to accomplish. Whether you're selling life insurance or lingerie, promoting your medical or legal practice, or any other venture, if you can't hold your customer's attention, you're not going to close most deals.

A life insurance salesperson is constantly distracted with a variety of personal problems. Unable to focus her attention, she often loses interest in conversations, drifting from one subject to another. Her clients get frustrated with her inability to maintain consistent focus on a specific subject. After many futile attempts, she finally gets a chance to submit a lucrative proposal to a wealthy prospect. During the meeting she speaks out:

"Dr. Jones, so we finally get to meet. You look a lot younger than the voice I've heard on the telephone. It's a pleasure to finally get in front of each other [so far so good]. Now, I've got this wonderful guaranteed renewable, level-term policy with no proof of insurability. In your position, there's no need for cash value or risky non-forfeiture provisions. My rates can't be beat. This will provide your family with all the protection they need during these vulnerable years at an unbelievable price. Now, how does that sound to you?"

Looking a little puzzled, the busy physician says:

"Sally, I'm not sure what you mean by some of these things. Do you think you could explain some of the terms and conditions?

With her pager going off, she asks Dr. Jones, "Do you mind if I use your phone to make a local call . . . it won't be but just a minute." She proceeds to make her call and is placed on hold. While on hold jotting down some notes on a legal tablet she finds on Dr. Jones' desk, she says:

"So, you have some questions about the policy. There's really nothing to be concerned about--it's all boiler-plate. Let me see . . . [someone gets on the other end of the phone] Dr. Jones I'll be with you in just a minute. Marv, how's it going? When did you say they'd be done installing the granite in the kitchen? We've got to meet to look at faucets and appliances. You really think it's absolutely necessary to have the Subzero? It's so damn expensive! What do you think?"

Noticing Dr. Jones' growing impatience, Sally abruptly ends her call. Attempting to salvage the meeting, she says:

"So . . . anyway, what do you think of that level-term policy? We could try some variable, universal life where you could do your own asset allocation . . ."

By this time Dr. Jones was already so disgusted with Sally's insensitive lack of attention that he just tuned her out. Overdosing prospective clients with insurance mumbo-jumbo is bad enough, but when Dr. Jones sought some clarification and was given a ration of inattention about her 'remodel' that was enough for him. Common sense tells you when you're engaged in any activity involving another person's attention, you'd better remain somewhat focused.

Lacking eye contact was the minor infraction compared with inappropriately using some one else's time to shoot the breeze with your contractor. Losing interest and looking distracted was taken by Dr. Jones as a slap in the face. There's far too many people hitting on him to make this kind of mistake more than once. Although we don't have to be psychic to speculate about the outcome, in most sales and social situations you don't get the luxury of a second chance.

Energy's in Short Supply

High energy and charisma go together like fizz and soda pop. Without it, you have a flat, unappealing product regardless of the package. Some people are overflowing with energy while others can't buy it for any price. One thing is clear, if you're 'low-energy' your charisma is going to be frozen like an Eskimo Pie. Demonstrating high energy generates the kind of warmth which invites healthy relating. When it's missing, otherwise socially gregarious people can be made to look lethargic and boring.

It's one thing to communicate clearly, it's still another to lose your energy. Energy provides a forgiving margin of safety to most interactions. It's truly a universal language which carries a message with added clout. Regardless of how ineptly you communicate, exuding energy gets your message across, despite the fact that you may not have articulated yourself perfectly. While your motivation may be good--namely, you have the desire to succeed--low energy creates the impression that you're disinterested and withdrawn.

For some people, energy is one of those ethereal qualities that comes and goes. When it goes, you feel the weight of gravity--everything seems uphill. When it's there, everything seems easy and effortless. Chasing this mercurial quality often leads people to experiment with many inexplicable things: Special diets, exotic nutritional supplements, psychoactive medications, romantic relationships, religious experiences, unique acquisitions, travel or any other activities or events in which this precious but fragile commodity might be reclaimed. Dousing yourself with coffee or seeking out various chemicals with which to capture this precious commodity, only makes matters worse.

Artificial supplies of energy, e.g., various types of stimulants, can only last so long and eventually run out. In fact, synthetic stimulants are known to build a strong tolerance in which you must consume dangerously high doses to attain a comparable effect. Eventually, you must accept the fact that you have to give up unnatural sources of energy. All lasting energy stems from either life or spiritual sources. Since the latter is beyond the scope of this book, it's the former over which you can assert some measure of control. Recognizing that life-force or sexual energy provides an abundant supply of drive, it's more than an important discovery: It's your hidden, but inexhaustible gold mine.

Some people find this a frightening discovery--scary because many people are told that it's morally incorrect or even dangerous. Actually, not discovering the use of this untapped well is more dangerous since its denial is known to cause unpredictable episodes. When you make friends with and get to know your life-force, you'll realize it's an invaluable source of motivation. Without this recognition, it's left to unexpected eruptions at work or elsewhere. Having access to this renewable source of inspiration, affords the energy to pursue a number of important goals. As long as the life-force is channeled into targeted goals, it remains at your disposal. If it's denied or dismissed, it remains lurking around ready for spontaneous discharge in perhaps inappropriate or counterproductive ways. Many self-defeating unconscious acts are attributable to ignoring this powerful source of verve and vigor.

Controlling this source of endless drive represents an important step in developing charisma and relating successfully. When ordinary communication is filtered with this type of energy it takes on a new life with unanticipated excitement. Not transfusing your communications with this special essence leaves your audience uninspired and unimpressed. Whether you're a tele-evangelist, physician, salesperson, politician, corporate player, student or anything else, your capacity to relate and connect with people is paralyzed without this vital essence. Allowing yourself to (a) acknowledge its existence and (b) channel it into your various activities, will create levels of charisma and powerful relating not yet experienced.

A young, ambitious corporate executive in the movie business has climbed to the top in record time. A jealous colleague with whom he attended film school complains about watching his lively friend blow by him. While discussing where he's gone wrong with one of his friends, he can't quite figure out his buddy's secret formula. Of course, he's really interested in finding the magic potion for himself. He's just clueless about what he's missing. Sounding incredulous and a tad envious, he remarks:

"Cindy, it's just amazing. How the hell did David do it? He's now been promoted [shaking his head] to president of the studio? I don't get it! We went to the same film school at the same time. He always counted on me for help. His projects weren't that creative and his grades were mediocre. What gives? I know he's great with the ladies, but that shouldn't count for anything--right? He even had to repeat his finance classes. What's going on?"

His friend Cindy, a production executive at the same studio, has also known David for some time. She's been most impressed with his abundant energy and lively personality. Trying to put his meteoric rise at the studio into perspective, she says:

"Morry, I totally understand your frustration. Let's face it, David's got it! Even though he's using Minoxidil, there's something about him--he's just sexy. Have you ever seen the way he looks at you? You know what I mean . . . it's like he's 'interested' in you or something. Oh, don't get me wrong, he's never tried to come on to me or anything. But, it's sort of like he's just interested. Anyway, everyone likes him--you can't help wanting to be around him. He's exciting. You just feel better being around him. He's always so complimentary. He just has great energy!"

Looking incredulous and beginning to get the picture, Morry remarks:

"Gee whiz . . . sounds to me like he's got you hook, line and sinker. I think he's the best smoke blower in the business--and that's why he's where he is. You know how many times he misfired when he's selected creative projects? Plenty! It's amazing to me how easily he's off the hook. Because he's got that something 'special,' he's the lucky one. Look, I know you 'like' the guy, but wouldn't you rather want the big business decisions in someone else's hands? I know I would. Whatever!"

"Morry, I know you're right in certain ways. But I wouldn't want to report to anyone other than David. Although he doesn't know everything, I find him hysterical, fun and approachable. He's never pulled rank on me or made me feel inferior in any way. That has to count for something in my book. I really like having him as my boss . . ."

As you can see, charisma isn't a logical thing. When someone has it, many of their otherwise noticeable faults are easily forgiven. And yet putting a finger on those special qualities is sometimes like looking for a needle in a haystack. Morry's frustration stems, at least in part, from the fact that *he* doesn't have much charisma. He can't, for the life of him, figure out why people are drawn to David like moths to a light. His abundant energy, his sex appeal, his willingness to share his personality, his positive approach with people, etc., all combine to make him irresistible.

Although he has his own limitations, they're easily forgiven. Talking about his faults or deficiencies falls on deaf ears. Unlike his jealous associate, David knows how to relate. Unfortunately for Morry, he doesn't. David connects and bonds well with people and they crave his company. Using his life-force to enhance the lives of others, he doesn't exploit people sexually or in other ways, but capitalizes on his expanded influence by enlisting their support, hard work and loyalty.

By spreading this desexualized [not directed toward sexual behavior] energy through his various activities, David is able to energize his environment and develop creative outlets. He makes himself exciting and attractive to others. His charisma and relating skills enable him to attain levels of success not available to those with less evolved interpersonal skills. While Morry prefers to attribute David's success to *luck*, the truth is that it's related to his energy level and other *high-level intangibles*.

Dissipating this coveted energy on compensatory sexuality, alcohol or drugs, gambling, excessive entertainment and other unproductive indulgences tragically squanders this priceless asset. As we've seen, spending too much time engaged is self-stimulation is the poison pill to success. Put another way, narcissism--or extreme vanity and self-obsession--prevents you from sharing this magnetic energy with others. As long as your energy is wasted on yourself or expended on other indulgences, you won't be developing charisma.

Most narcissistic preoccupations prevent individuals from relating to others and interfere with developing charismatic abilities. Charisma is very strongly linked to transcending narcissism and redirecting energy toward others and creative activities. Burning up energy on various forms of self-stimulation not only short circuits relating but mortally wounds charismatic talents.

Sexualized energy must be transformed into a host of creative ventures. Whether you're selling cars, writing screenplays, playing sports, treating patients, trading securities or any other venture, charisma requires directing your energy into constructive channels. If you've wasted yourself with excessive self-indulgence, you can't expect to give lavishly to anyone else. As long as you're preoccupied with your own pleasure seeking, relating to others won't come easily. By spending less energy on yourself, you'll have a lot more reserves to develop meaningful relationships.

Engaging friends and influencing people is very much related to sharing intense energy with others. It's unrealistic to talk about giving others attention when you're consumed with being the center of attention. By not monopolizing the need for attention and directing your energy toward others, you'll create strong bonds and develop powerful levels of charisma.   Unloading too much sexual energy directly, namely, chasing too many 'fantasies,' handicaps your communication and socialization skills.

Whether you're dissipating your energy engaging in compensatory sexuality, e.g., compulsive affairs or 'self-abuse' or acting overly seductive, it's going to dilute your relating abilities and charisma.   Without intensifying and transferring sexual energy, efforts at communication and relating lack impact and pizzazz.   When it's present, communication is highly charged and filled with electricity and excitement.

Charismatic people relate effectively by comfortably wearing their sexuality on their sleeves.   It's not like they're deliberately seductive or have ulterior motives.   But they're engaging and playful.   Flirting with lively, animated conversations,   charismatic   people   are   filled   with enthusiasm.   Whether they're talking about mundane business matters or banal personal relationships, charismatic people are brimming with excitement.   No matter how routine   things   seem,   they're   always   exploring   new developments with interest and eagerness.   Charging neutral situations   with   sexualized   energy   automatically   elevates routine   situations   into   stimulating   adventures.   By displaying high levels of energy, routinely banal activities are instantly transformed into new and exciting events.

Words Do Matter

Words or language makes or breaks a person's ability to relate and get charisma.   While we'd like to believe that only intentions count, the truth is that the specific words used in communication have a huge impact.   How you say things does matter. *High-level intangibles*, like tact, diplomacy, timing, 'common sense,' and good judgment, make or break your charisma. Speaking in ways comfortable to you but either arcane or objectionable to others won't help your cause. Harboring expectations that everyone knows what you mean--mind reading--is misleading and often leads to predictable disappointments.

While most people don't deliberately set out to confuse or offend others, there's a wide semantic gap between most people. Good communicators use *high-level intangibles* and find special ways of bridging this abyss and getting through to their audiences. In most business or social situations, if your audience doesn't 'get it' then you're most likely going to miss an opportunity. Since relating involves a delicate mixture of language and interpersonal skills, it pays to get it right the first time around. Making too many clumsy mistakes can be costly and maybe irreversible.

Most people are impressed with sophisticated vocabulary, especially if it distinguishes you from the crowd. Using creative language--by selecting unique and effective vocabulary--has a powerful charismatic effect. On the other hand, appearing overly mundane or too folksy can boomerang by making you look sloppy or unintelligent. Without appearing pedantic, charismatic people use language in ways which communicate and create bonded relationships.

Applying creative and descriptive vocabulary is one of the easiest ways to appear informed and intelligent, as long as you don't overdo it. Pushing too hard to appear 'brilliant' by using excessively big words can easily backfire. Stringing together overly 'sophisticated' language creates an awkward and pretentious presentation. Verbal communication is an art-form which requires balance, moderation, tact and timing. Charismatic language incorporates a healthy blend of colloquial or folksy expressions together with carefully timed sophisticated vocabulary.

A charismatic defense attorney, known for his powerful evangelical oratory, addresses a jury in a sensational murder trial. Despite his 'Ivy League' education, he deliberately speaks to the jury in pedestrian terms, making his best efforts to connect on their level. Adjusting his language to fit the jury, he speaks to them in their own vernacular. Showing his folksy side, he communicates in their language but occasionally flashes his upscale education. Attempting to influence their perceptions of the police, he says [with evangelical intensity]:

"Y'awl are fix'n to look at the facts. The police's version makes no sense. *You can't trust the messenger*! You must send an *unambiguous* message to the police: They can't violate your civil liberties. It's their time to pay for breaking the law. You, in this jury, are commissioned with the responsibility of preserving our cherished constitutional guarantees. *If it* [the evidence] *doesn't fit, you must acquit.* Only you can send the police the message that 'we, the people,' won't tolerate this *egregious* abuse of their authority!"

Communicating deliberately in folksy ways, the attorney attempts to establish an immediate bond with his audience. His familiar, non-threatening tone opens the door to receptivity, but his 'sophisticated' vocabulary asserts his authority and credibility. Using catchy slogans, e.g., *"You can't trust the messenger"* or *"If it doesn't fit, you must acquit"* also sends an unforgettable message to the jury. Since his goal is acquittal for his client, he cleverly distracts the jury from examining the evidence and, instead, admonishes them to fulfill their constitutional duty by sending an unequivocal message to the police: Acquittal. By incorporating familiar language, using powerful metaphorical expressions, and applying judicious amounts of 'sophisticated' vocabulary, charismatic relating has been expanded considerably.

Transferring positive energy is also a necessary step for relating effectively and developing charismatic communication. But without choosing your words wisely, it won't be enough to get results. Saying 'what's the bottom line?,' doesn't short-circuit the need to communicate in ways which build rapport and create relationships. While no one wants to waste time and avoid getting down to business, there's a necessary courtship or engagement required in most business or social situations. There's no excuse for rudeness or abruptness. When you revert to intolerance in conversations, it's a sure sign that you'll hurt your charisma. Taking a strategic approach in which you're making your best efforts to attain your objectives goes a long way in avoiding pitfalls in relating. Despite your frustration, it's unrealistic and counterproductive to impatiently demand:

- "OK, what's your bottom line . . .?," or

- "Let's cut to the chase . . .," or

- "Enough of this idle chatter, what do you really want . . .?," or even more obnoxious,

- "Stop wasting my time, make your point . . ."

Confrontational statements like these put too much pressure on the second party in the communication and usually lead to defensiveness and antagonism.   And if you're causing acrimony, you're inadvertently hurting your ability to relate and reducing your charisma.   Accelerating the relating process by 'cutting to the chase' often makes a doable situation unlikely and untenable.   Relating takes deliberation,   calculation,   patience   and   execution   in otherwise mundane conversations to succeed.   You know you're not succeeding when the second party cuts you off. This type of communication failure is avoidable most of the time.   Rather than showing impatience, find creative ways to keep conversations going.

When a conversation 'dies,' you're doing something wrong or, at least, not paying close attention to important cues.   All conversations involve certain cues or signals telling you in which direction to go.   Tuning-in to these cues helps redirect your efforts to put the conversation back on the right track. If a person folds their arms and remains silent [obvious body language], it usually indicates a sign of defensiveness or that you're heading in the wrong direction.   Noting this, it's sometimes helpful to either make simple observations or statements   or   ask   a   non-threatening   question   for clarification.   For   most   people   questions   come   more naturally and can bail you out.   When phrasing questions, try asking them in respectful and conditional language [the italics indicate conditional emphasis]:

- *"Forgive* me for asking, but *would* you mind . . . ?," or

- "Is it *possible* that you *might* . . . ?," or

- "I'm *sorry* to *trouble* you, but I *wonder* if . . . ?," or

- *"Could* I *impose* on you for . . . ?," or

- "I *wonder* if it's *possible* that . . .?," or

- "With your *permission*, *would* it be *possible* that . . .?"

By prefacing your questions with tentative, respectful language you're much less likely to register objections. After all, objections are going to occur regardless of how smooth you are at communicating. But when they do, they can be softened--just a little--by asking questions in less offensive ways. If you're still finding yourself getting limited results by asking questions, turning a question inside-out makes it a non-threatening statement. That's really the only difference between asking questions and making direct statements. Simply invert the subject and the predicate by saying: "Are *you* feeling . . . , ?" OR "You *are* feeling . . ." The former's a question and the latter's a statement.

Sometimes hazarding your observations or making statements keeps conversation going better than asking questions. Asking questions--no matter how respectfully phrased--can create an atmosphere of interrogation leading the second party to become defensive or 'clam up.' Like tentatively phrased questions, conditional statements are good first-aid in keeping conversations alive. They also have the advantage of eliciting responses not otherwise obvious in the course of normal conversations [italics also indicate respectful or conditional language]:

- "You *seem* like you're . . ." or

- "I get the *impression* that you *might* . . ." or

- "*Perhaps* you *might* be the type that likes . . ." or

- "It's *possible* that a *part* of you *might* . . ." or

- "It seems '*as if*' you think there *might* be . . ." or

- "*Forgive* me for taking your time, but I know . . ."

Remember, words can be perceived as weapons or powerful tools. By gently using these phrases, individuals are more inclined to react with less defensiveness or opposition. When you're caught putting words in peoples' mouths and jumping to conclusions it's more difficult to deal with objections. Certainly making any statements which antagonize your audience only hurts your prospects of advancing your cause. Couching statements in conditional language helps soften the blow of soliciting sensitive information or imparting unwanted ideas. Showing awareness of your audience's 'hot-buttons' helps circumvent problems before they occur. At the very least, doing your utmost to phrase things in non-offensive ways goes a long way in keeping open otherwise dead-end conversations.

A life insurance salesman is having considerable difficulty closing a large deal with his obstreperous client. Although he's presented all the facts and figures, his client continues to harbor significant objections blocking the sale. While the client accepts the basic premise of purchasing life insurance, the salesman still finds himself having difficulty closing the deal. At yet another meeting trying to close his client, the salesman comments:

"Bill, you'll be a lot better off with this variable life policy. It gives you the flexibility of allocating the types of investments you'd like to have with the cash-value portion of the policy. I know this is the right plan for you. You're the type of person who likes to remain in control of every situation. What could be more perfect than you remaining in control of how your cash-value is invested. I knew this would be right for you. Don't you think this is a perfect match? You're not going to get a better deal from anyone else."

Reacting to Sam's decisive comments, Bill says:

"Sam, I know *you* think this is the best plan for me. But what about me. You're so sure of yourself--but I'm not! How can you be so certain, when I'm still trying to figure out what's best for me? It's amazing how you know more than I do. At least I'm trying to figure out what's best for me. Besides which, how can you possibly say I'm not going to get a better deal from anyone else? You don't know who I've been talking to."

Not yet recognizing the value of tentative and conditional language, Sam continues to hammer away at his client:

"Look Bill, I've been selling life insurance for some time. I've reviewed all the policies and matched up your needs with what policies are available. I've actually plugged your demographic data into the computer and it's given me the exact policy which best fits your needs. Now you're not going to argue with the computer are you? Obviously our rates are competitive with everyone else. I'm not going to be undersold. I know you're not going to find a better program for your situation."

Continuing to find objections to Sam's imperious approach, Bill remarks:

"Sam, you might be right about what you're saying. But I'm not yet prepared to make any decisions. I'm still looking at other options including term insurance. What's wrong with term insurance? I've been told it's a lot more affordable."

From the dialogue we can see that Sam's going nowhere with his client. He's just not relating. His presumptuous approach has created unnecessary antagonism by forcefully telling Bill what he wants. While the salesman is giving it his best shot, there's virtually no use of conditional language. Instead, he sounds opinionated and imperious. Clearly, he's turned Bill off and reduced his chances of ever closing the deal. Taking a more respectful approach in which Sam couches his statements in tentative, conditional language offers the possibility of not repeating this fatal mistake with his next client. Most people don't get the luxury of undoing the damage. After making costly mistakes, damage control strategies are known to yield unpredictable results. First impressions--whether positive of negative--are often lasting and are stubbornly resistant to change.

A more enlightened Sam, having learned the value of carefully choosing his words, might start over by saying [conditional and respectful language italicized]:

"Bill, I *wonder* if the policy we discussed *seems* to address your needs. There *might* be other options to take depending on you goals. If I *could* be permitted, *please* allow me to share with you some other insurance plans. It's *possible* that one of these policies *might* better serve your needs. *Forgive* me for taking too much of your time, but *perhaps* we'll come up with the right formula."

Without being a rocket scientist, it's safe to say that Sam would make more progress by imparting his proposal with respectful and conditional language. Although words aren't exactly verbal magic, the right words can have magical effects. Certainly using presumptuous language risks offending and alienating your audience. But incorporating conditional language goes a long way in keeping the doors of communication open. Even if it doesn't persuade Bill to make the purchase, using diplomatic language keeps the conversation alive.

Regardless of the venue, adopting diplomatic language helps circumvent self-inflicted wounds. It's difficult enough to overcome objections and persuade people to your way of thinking; but if you're hurting your own cause by acting in onerous ways that's truly inexcusable. By simply incorporating conditional and respectful language, your relating skills will leave you one important step closer to developing charisma.

Validation is the Magic Key

Validation is the process by which you give approval and reinforce an individuals' self-esteem. It usually takes the form of directly positive statements known as compliments. When properly administered, it's one of the most powerful tools of interpersonal relating. Using it lavishly dramatically expands one's charisma. In case you're wondering, validation is diametrically opposed to criticism and has the effect of motivating people to pursue their personal best. It's the surest interpersonal tool with which to award approval.

In many ways, validation and approval are more powerful than money. Nothing motivates more than patting someone on the back. Money's a powerful reward but it pales in comparison to the impact of approval. Like a tempting dessert, there's always a little more room for approval.

Unlike money, only approval can motivate people to pursue their personal best--in whatever arena.

Criticism, on the other hand, has limited and even destructive motivational effects. Although some people are temporarily motivated to avoid the sting of criticism, it doesn't have lasting benefits. It punishes a person by attacking their pride and self-worth, and has the effect of usurping precious energy and motivation. Nothing detracts more from inspiring peak performance than encountering criticism and disapproval. Regardless of the venue, approval usually remains in short supply. Criticism, like used cars, is far more ubiquitous: It follows the laws of gravity and rolls downhill. Blaming and criticism comes far more naturally to most people. Learning the art of validation is a labor-intensive process which pays endless rewards. With a little practice, its payoffs are staggering!

Validation varies from person to person but generally involves acknowledging something special about a person which elevates their self-esteem. It might be a positive statement about their looks, personality, work, creativity, morality, relationship or any other significant aspect of a person's life. Finding what's validating to a person is the key to winning their enduring loyalty and support. Diagnosing this need enables individuals to fill a private void for which they're eternally grateful. It also provides a measure of leverage in social and business situations. When you control a person's source of validation and approval, you're in a powerful position.

Most people crave compliments and flattery but rarely have the good fortune of capturing them. Faced with a daily ration of criticism and rejection, they seek and crave individuals who lavishly dole out praise and compliments. Developing mastery at delivering validation creates instant popularity. Anyone who asserts that 'flattery will get your nowhere,' obviously has seldom been the recipient of praise and compliments. If they had, they'd also be chasing after compliments like a magical elixir. Examples of using validation and approval are manifold:

- "You're so intelligent . . . ," or

- "That was an excellent point . . . ," or

- "I just love your taste . . .," or

- "You're extremely attractive/handsome/beautiful/ sexy . . .," or

- "I've never met anyone like you . . . ," or

- "You're the most special person I've ever met . . ."

Statements like these are intravenous feeding to one's self-esteem and creates an immediate and enduring bond. Regardless of their accuracy, these kinds of statements generate instant feelings of liking and attraction. Many love relationships develop from one's experience of being around a sumptuous amount of approval and validation. At the other extreme and far more frequent are individuals whose life-experience has dealt them a heavy dose of rejection and criticism. Constant criticism breeds dislike, resentment and self-contempt. If unchecked, self-contempt leads to hostility and a host of retaliatory actions, including, drug and alcohol abuse, compulsive eating, aberrant sex, and lying, predictable patterns of self-defeating behavior and even suicide.

A talented and ambitious musician is attempting to advance his career. Forced to rely heavily on managers, agents, publicists and various handlers, he constantly feels misled and disappointed. Having his expectations raised to unrealistic levels, he frequently goes through a roller-coaster ride in which he expects to have the rug pulled from underneath him. While at a power breakfast with his agent he expresses some of his frustrations:

"You know Mel, I'm really getting tired of all the empty promises. How long am I expected to wait to land the latest record deal? You're constantly telling me, 'chill,' 'be patient,' 'it takes time,' 'it's in the bag . . .' All I see you doing is spending time promoting your teenage 'phenoms.' You seem to deliver for them, why not me? Maybe you're jaded or something. I just can't stand waiting anymore."

Feeling ambushed and unfairly criticized, his agent Angelo says:

"Mel, get real! Do you have a clue how many heavy hitters have heard your 'demo.' I know you'd like to see something happen . . . so would I. But, for whatever reason, it's just not happening at the moment. Believe me, it's in the right hands, but I can't break their arms. Forget what's happening to any of my other clients . . . they shouldn't concern you. You should wish them the best and only hope that the same thing happens to you."

Although the agent's response is defensive in its tone, it does help place Mel's frustrations into perspective. But Mel's critical response does very little to continue encouraging his agent to work hard on his behalf. Instead, it brow beats him for not doing enough. Whatever the realities, Mel's goal ought to be motivating his, agent not making him feel his job is a thankless task. By thinking strategically, containing his frustrations, and validating his agent he'd be in a lot better position to orchestrate his agenda. Flashing his cards and unloading negativity--while providing temporary relief--only makes matters worse. A more savvy musician, armed with the strategic advantages of validation, gets another shot at the conversation:

"Hey Angelo, how's it going? How's the wife and family? I hope everything is going well. Anyway . . . I guess no news is good news. You've done a great job getting the tape in the right hands. You're the man! There's no one better than you to represent my work. I just have to realize it's going to happen when it's going to happen. And that's it! I just want to let you know how grateful I am for believing in my work. You're the best!"

Although perhaps a bit overdone, Mel's second go around is far more encouraging than his first. Rather than blaming him, expressing appreciation is bound to endear himself to his most valuable friend--his agent. By learning the art of validation, Mel's in a much better position to eventually achieve his goals. His more mature perspective enables him to control his frustrations and keep the doors open for this and future projects.

Presenting negative responses only makes difficult situations worse. Giving his agent--who might actually be somewhat negligent or at least focused on other projects--a face-saving way out by offering another plausible explanation, namely, that "it's going to happen when it's going to happen," is a productive strategy. Blaming him for incompetent management usurps his agent's motivation and guarantees that he won't be working too hard on his behalf. Taking the higher ground, showing tact and diplomacy, and administering a healthy dose of validation can only help matters improve.

Related to validation is the notion of showing empathy:
Making someone believe that you're 'walking in their
shoes.' It's the opposite of narcissism in which blinding
selfishness stops individuals from extending themselves to
others. Unlike narcissism, empathy accelerates
interpersonal relating and charisma. Empathy is conveyed
in many ways including, (a) showing undivided attention,
(b) listening without interrupting, maintaining good eye
contact, (c) rendering supportive comments and (d)
administering positive validation.

Showing empathy is an integral feature to effective relating
and an essential component of charisma. Together with
validation, it's a powerful source of personal persuasion and
influence. Without it, your ability to work your way into
key positions is severely compromised. With it, you'll earn
loyalty and command the leadership to orchestrate your
personal agenda. Empathy allows you to develop a solid
bond with your audience improving relating and charisma in
many unexpected ways.

Empathy and validation help *Teflon*-proof the personality
by creating enduring, loyal relationships. It's difficult to
attack or discredit people with whom you have close
personal ties. There's just too much guilt. Showing
sensitivity and consideration is a great preemptive strategy
against personal attacks. Conversely, disparaging others--
regardless of the rationale--usually backfires and invites
almost immediate retaliation. How do you justify
dismantling someone who's made special efforts to show
you sensitivity and consideration? It's far easier to attack
narcissistic individuals whose ruthless insensitivity and
arrogance bulldozes everyone in their path. By abandoning
callous self-centeredness and directing your attention and
energy toward helping others, you'll be far more immune to

personal attacks. When someone's beating their chest and lording over their self-deluded claims of superiority, it's easy to find fault and become vindictive.

Regardless of your walk of life, empathy demonstrates the kind of awareness and sensitivity necessary for building new and enduring relationships. Few people tire of empathic individuals; just as certainly they grow weary all too quickly of their narcissistic counterparts. Using empathy is also essential to developing strong business and social relationships. No matter how shaky the deal and tenuous the relationships, using empathy and validation can turn an otherwise risky situation into a positive outcome.

An aspiring young actress is striking out trying to find an agent. Although many of her friends have agents, she's tried to gain representation with little effect. She's consistently told that if she gets more acting 'gigs' under her belt, she won't have any trouble signing on. Until then, no one's interested. Faced with the dilemma, she asks one of her successful friends from acting class how she got started. Sipping a mochacino at Starbucks following acting class, she complains:

"Mary, I'm caught between a rock and a hard place. I can't get acting work because I don't have an agent . . . and I can't get an agent because I haven't worked. I'm in a real catch-22. I just don't know what direction to take. What did you do to get started?"

Remembering all too well how difficult it was to gain representation, Mary showed some genuine interest in helping. Nibbling on a biscotti, she says:

"Julia, I totally understand your frustration. I was faced with that exact situation. Let me tell you what I did. You know Maggie, don't you? She also goes to Len's acting class. You probably haven't seen much of her lately because she's always on location somewhere. When I was getting started she invited me to a Sunday brunch where I got to meet her agent. After hitting it off, he decided to take me on as a client . . . and the rest is history. You know . . . I'm having my agent over next Sunday and I'll invite you. How does that sound?"

Showing a little nervousness, Julia says:

"Really? What happens if he doesn't like me. I mean . . . I don't know what I'd say. What do you think I should wear? Do you think I should be sexy or conservative? I mean, I don't want him to think I'm a flake. You know him best; what do you think?"

Sensing Julia's concerns, Maggie comments:

"Don't be silly--you'll be fine! Len's a great guy. He's really easy to talk to because he's a non-stop talker--a real yenta. All you have to do is act like a shrink: Just pay close attention, nod, listen and reframe. Try to get him to talk about his Lalique collection--it's his passion. It's really that easy. You're one of the easiest people I know to talk to. You're going to do great!"

While sipping some Asti-Spumante at the brunch, Maggie finally gets around to introducing Julia and Len. Sharing some important trivialities, Julie says:

"Len, Maggie really thinks the world of you. You've helped develop her career--I'm sure you've done that for a number of people. I understand you're into collecting Lalique. I just love Lalique. I can't think of any crystal more sensual and glamorous."

"Nice meeting you Julia. Oh, you like Lalique too? I just picked up an original piece of R. Lalique from the '20s. It's a perfume bottle in dark blue with stars all over bottle. It's just exquisite. It's such a challenge finding these rare old pieces. It's like capturing a piece of a bygone era. I just love the art deco period of the '30s and '40s. How about you?"

Responding to Len's enthusiasm, Julia says:

"That's really fantastic. I only have new pieces that I've bought at Macy's. It takes a lot of sophistication and patience to chase after R. Lalique pieces. How did you get started collecting R. Lalique? You must have a real artistic side to you.

Happy to share his favorite pastime, Len goes on:

"Actually, it's funny. I was at a trade show in Los Angeles and at the convention center was a R. Lalique exhibit. Ever since then, I've been obsessed. Apart from my clients, it keeps me busy. Now did you say you're looking for an agent? I'm always looking to represent the right kind of talent. You've got a great look--and a personality to go with it. Why don't you call my secretary next week and schedule an appointment. I don't have my organizer on me."

Now whether Len ever took on Julia we can't be certain, but it's safe to say that tuning-in to his interests, demonstrating empathy and validating his narcissism, left Len a lot more drawn to Julia. Had Julia been obsessed and imposed upon Len with her own eccentric interests, the conversation might have sank under its own weight. Proving herself to be a quick-study, Julia learned that becoming a scintillating conversationalist was as simple as letting Len do all the talking. Although he liked her validation, he *loved* the fact that she was a good listener and paid him undivided attention.

Responding energetically to someone else's needs and interests offers a far higher return on one's investment than engaging in narcissistic exhibitionism. Anyone's capable of monopolizing conversations with their own idiosyncratic interests. But it takes a person of considerable foresight and refinement to strategically address someone else's needs. By remaining focused--as her friend Maggie suggested--on Len's interests, Julia made a lot more progress than had she dominated the conversation with her own obsessions.

Showing empathy and validation creates an instant relationship which automatically elevates a person's self-esteem. Together with avoiding critical remarks, using this approach is a powerful combination for developing charisma and shaping all types of behavior. Whether you're seeking a promotion, influencing a jury, making a sale, acquiring a bigger diamond ring or hoping for a benefit of the doubt in any other arena involving human beings, you can always count on empathy and validation to get the job done.

Humor's a Great Defense

A good sense of humor is an essential component of charisma and effective relating. With life's many strenuous detours, humor offers an opportunity to put things in perspective. It's like a shock absorber smoothing out the many bumps in the road. By enabling people to adjust better to life's many challenges, it's an effective coping mechanism. Without humor, dealing with ordinary events is more stressful. With humor, stressful events are reinterpreted in a positive context. Finding a silver-lining to life's many disappointments isn't a matter of just using better rationalizations or making feeble excuses, it's a matter of survival.

Faced with failure and defeat, maintaining a sense of humor improves many aspects of adversity, keeping people on the right track. With too much disappointment and failure comes discouragement, anger and maybe depression. Taking things too seriously invites a self-defeating pattern of negativity, leading to bad results. Humor provides a protective buffer cushioning many of life's unexpected blows. Absorbing too much adversity usurps positive energy, motivation and ambition. And when you're depleted of your energy, pursuing even the most inconsequential goals becomes an uphill battle.

Using humor is about maintaining perspective, keeping motivation, searching for new solutions and learning many unanticipated lessons. Humor adds to the resiliency of personality by protecting the ego from devastation. In fact, with individuals having difficulty coping, their sense of humor is usually one of the first things to go. And along with it goes the ability to learn from experience. Humorless people are usually so defensive that they barricade themselves in their own protective world. Attempting to avoid pain and suffering, they're insulated from learning new ways of adapting to life. What's tragic is the fact that they're also prevented from developing new sources of opportunity and satisfaction.

Like most narcissistic wounds, withdrawal from a painful world prevents individuals from learning important lessons of life. Without a healthy sense of humor, counterproductive options are sometimes taken. When something is taken too 'seriously,' it's a good bet that a person no longer has a functional sense of humor. Under enough stress and missing this defense mechanism, individuals are more prone toward substance abuse, sexual acting-out, angry outbursts, violent behavior, depression and even suicide. Without a healthy layer of humor, individuals find themselves easily threatened and emotionally labile.

Unable to protect themselves against common insults, individuals with a dysfunctional sense of humor often take things the wrong way. They're too easily insulted when others dismiss innocuous comments as facetious or amusing. Like beauty, humor is also in the eye of the beholder, because what's humorous to one person might be offensive to another. When one's ego is in a weakened state--due to heightened stress and a loss of humor--ordinarily harmless remarks can be misinterpreted leading to paranoia and even rage reactions. Other things being equal, many ballistic episodes are due to a failed sense of humor and exaggerated emotional reactions. Without a well developed sense of humor, relating and charisma are low on the food chain.

A physician at a prestigious university teaching hospital, whose poverty stricken Appalachien upbringing was well known and whose knowledge of radiation therapy was considered unsurpassed, is presiding over his weekly triage meeting, Having been kidded for being a hillbilly, he shows 'seismographic' sensitivity to his background. During the meeting, a playful nurse, whose own blue-blood background was also well known, likes poking fun at Dr. White's down-home accent. Trying to get his goat, she says:

"Dr. White, when you're instructing us to y'awl come down yonder because 'om fix'n to show you . . .' I guess you're going to give a demonstration of something. Is that really what your mean?"

Overreacting to her playful remarks in front of the group, he quips:

"Ms. Marks [raising his voice loudly], if you're having trouble following my instructions I would suggest you take better notes. I've noticed lately that you're having difficulty absorbing things. Maybe we should send you down to audiology for a hearing check! Or maybe it's time for a transfer to a different department."

Sensing that she's pushed him over the edge, Nurse Marks responds:

"Dr. White . . . you need to chill! I was just kidding. I find your accent rather charming. We all understand you--most of the time."

Still showing some huffiness, Dr. White says:

"All right [hastily exiting the conference room], that'll be it for today."

The fact that Dr. White has reacted in a mildly hostile manner flashes some of his ego-weakness and sensitivity to the group. Although Nurse Marks' remarks were somewhat offensive, Dr. White's bereft sense of humor made matters worse. Reacting as he did discloses his vulnerability and creates the impression that he's hyper-sensitive and not fully in charge. It's difficult to show leadership or control over any group, no matter what size, when you're so over-reactive to inconsequential provocations. Good management requires that you're capable of absorbing minor social infractions without exhibiting erratic behavior. Certainly Dr. White exercised some restraint by not resorting to expletives or going ballistic, but his unnecessary threat about 'transferring' Nurse Marks was uncalled for and exposes his weakness.

Rolling with the punches, having a better sense of humor and showing some personal confidence would be far better than exposing your sensitivities. It doesn't show much class to allow your subordinates to get under your skin. At the same time, had Dr. White shown more playfulness and a better sense of humor, he wouldn't have compromised his position of authority to the group. After all, the group has now seen his vulnerable side and is inclined to tiptoe around his soft-spots. When you're in a position of leadership and your reputation is on the line, it's preferable to not show any weakness unless it's intentional or for effect. Had Dr. White shown more playfulness and humor he might have responded differently to Nurse Marks' comments. Showing some playful hyperbole, he could have said:

"I guess I just ain't gett'n thru. Yes, 'om fix'n' to show you how the CT scan is properly operated . . .C'mon down!"

The added exaggeration would have introduced some levity into the situation and avoided a counterproductive dialogue exposing his humiliation and shame. Using more humor would have given him a better defense against his own vulnerability, helping him to remain in charge of future situations. Let's face it, sooner or later you're going to have to deal with some kind of insult or offensive remarks. It pays to be forearmed by honing your sense of humor.

A presidential candidate is engaged in a make or break nationally televised debate. With the election drawing near, he's running neck and neck with the incumbent. One wrong move or miscue could torpedo his chances. While holding his own with the president, he's asked an off-the-wall question by one of the interviewers:

"Mr. Dugan, during the campaign there's been considerable discussion about your advanced age and health. If you're elected, you'll be the oldest person ever to be elected president. Your opponent in this debate tonight has questioned whether you'd be able to manage the stress of the office and even complete a full term. Your program, which you've outlined tonight, calls for completion of two terms of office. My questions to you this evening: (1) Do you believe age and health are legitimate factors in this campaign? and (2) Do you plan to be a one-term president only?"

Smiling broadly and remaining collected, the voluble presidential candidate quips back:

"Mr. Walker, throughout this campaign I've made it plain-- I'm not going to exploit for political purposes my opponent's youth and inexperience."

With uproarious laughter heard in the gallery, the interviewer takes another shot:

"What about the your decision to run for a second term?"

The candidate warmly responds:

"Mr. Walker, about my health . . . I feel just fine. As for the other issue, we're still two weeks from election day. I think it would be a bit premature for me to be commenting about my second term before I've been elected to the first one. We'll just have to wait and see on that one."

Catching a few more laughs, the candidate met the test of using humor to defuse a potentially touchy situation. Had he reacted defensively and tried to justify his excellent health by citing his physician's reports, he would have drawn more attention to the issue and raised even more suspicions about his health. Responding effectively to questions doesn't mean answering them directly. Sometimes humor is the best response because it opens up an entirely new perspective. But there are also certain admonitions about using humor: There's a fine line between 'making fun' and being obnoxious. When you're the brunt of someone's jokes, it doesn't feel too good. Everyone has some areas in which they show certain sensitivities; and it's easy to unknowingly offend others.

To guard against this risk, it's safer to use self-deprecating humor--making yourself or your group or organization the brunt of the jokes. As with all humor, there's still a murky edge between showing levity and openly disclosing low self-esteem or even self-contempt. Self-effacing humor shouldn't be an open admission of how poorly you think of yourself, but instead a reminder that you're secure enough to laugh aloud about your foibles. It's easy to overdue humor either directed toward yourself or others. Appearing too sarcastic creates uneasiness because no one really knows where you're coming from or how to take you.

Over doing it leaves people running for cover, fearing that you might blurt out something which is acutely embarrassing. Excessive humor makes it difficult for people to also take you seriously and hurts your credibility. It does very little to enhance your ability to relate and display charisma. Recognizing when it's time to shut-off the humor is a valuable lesson. Regardless of the profession, most individuals require some credibility to transact any type of business. If you're not taken seriously, you'll be shooting yourself in the foot.

A well known comic is constantly joking with his business associates. Having great difficulty knowing when to say when, he's offended his agent and publicist to the point they want nothing to do with him. Although his audiences seem to laugh, his managers are disgusted with his non-stop vulgarities. At a recent meeting with his agent, he has trouble containing himself. Ventilating some of his frustrations about his lack of quality bookings, he says:

"Lenny, since when have you gotten so fat? What are you going to do . . . have bagels sewn into you Armani suits? I've got a great diet. Just pop some Viagra and douse yourself with Minoxidil. Your wife will love it! You're really looking good lately. Fat and bald is really in!"

Interrupting him, his agent tries to get him back on track and says:

"Don, you're really getting hard to take. Don't you ever stop with the cracks? Is it any wonder why you're playing Barstow now. I can't get you booked anywhere when people get to know you. You've really got to stop wisecracking. You're turning everyone off--including me. When are you going to learn? I know you've been told there's a difference between being 'funny' and obnoxious. Wake up, it's already getting late."

Like most substances, humor--used in moderation--can be an effective tool in relating and demonstrating charisma. When it's overdone, it's nothing short of falling on your own sword. While there's no guidebook on when to say when, tuning-in to your audience and showing some awareness lets you gauge what's acceptable and what's self-defeating. Clearly, if you're offending others it won't be long--whatever your situation--before you'll wind up in the ejection seat. Although it's helpful to use self-deprecating humor, it's also no guarantee that you won't hurt your cause. Appearing too self-effacing can also hurt your credibility by revealing self-contempt. At the same time, directing your humor toward others also requires responsible limits. When incorporated with other high-level intangibles, humor is an excellent tool to facilitate quality relating and charisma.

Altruism Is King

One of the most powerful features of charisma is controlling your own narcissism and dedicating yourself to multiplying the success of others. Charismatic people-- despite appearing vain and egocentric--place other people's needs before their own. They've learned that "private interest is best served by public interest," and if they devote themselves to improving the lives of others, their own success will multiply many fold. And this is the principle which drives altruistic people, not the fact that they're truly self-denying or self-sacrificing. In the evolution of the human race, surely no one really believes that worsening your situation is a preferred adaptation. No, the truth is that altruism is a strategy which yields beneficial results. Narcissism--or the philosophy of self-centeredness--begets diminished popularity, social isolation and rejection, and eventual failure.

Developing altruistic potential assures instant popularity by helping others to achieve their goals. Most people gravitate to individuals extending a helpful hand rather than grabbing everything in their path. The pyramid of success is always crowded at the bottom with an abundance of narcissists biting and scratching for their own survival. But only a few selected altruists can be found at the top. As we've said, it goes without saying that any successful individuals, in whatever the fields, have some narcissistic propensities propelling them toward success. But they've managed--despite their own neediness and greed--to orient themselves toward helping others because it pays rich rewards.

Altruism is seldom fashionable, at least in the large scheme of things, since most people are too busy focused on their own survival. For those pursuing the magic bullet of popularity and success, developing a healthy co-dependency or focusing on others' needs, is your safest bet. Most interpersonal success--whether it's in the politics of work or the family--involves 'following the leader.' Why do people really follow? They gravitate toward people whose association is bound to improve their situation. There's absolutely nothing more 'attractive' than connecting yourself to someone who's committed to improving your life. When others perceive you as focused on helping them succeed--in whatever ways are important to *them*--then they'll follow you with fierce loyalty.

Great leaders of today and the past have promised a better life, not to glorify themselves, but to improve the lot of their following. Can you imagine any leader--regardless of the enterprise--motivating people by saying, "Follow me so you can subsidize my extravagance and line my pockets." I don't think so. Even popular television ministries, whose leaders fleeced unsuspecting parishioners and whose lives were wildly extravagant, promised a better life to their followers. And that's how they became so popular. Politicians promising tax cuts, lower unemployment and more prosperity are displaying their altruistic commitments. But if the electorate catches the faint scent of self-serving motives, their popularity drops like a rock.

Charisma and effective interpersonal relating are highly dependent on conveying altruistic motives. True charisma is experiencing someone selflessly pursue the goal of helping others. Now whether, as we've seen, these altruistic demonstrations are motivated by personal greed, we can't be certain. But it's safe to say that orienting yourself around improving the lives of others, creates instant attraction to anyone following the path to success.

An ambitious, middle-aged, corporate executive in the film industry has been known to adopt stray actors struggling to make it in 'the business.' Frequently picking them up, or vice versa, while working-out at his fitness club, he does his best to land them minor parts in low-budget films in which his company is involved. Although there's nothing obvious in it for him, he still offers his help. His wife is especially upset by his tendency to lend them money when they have difficulty paying their bills. Over dinner she continues to voice her concerns:

"Jimmy, why do you waste your time hanging out with these losers? I know you like to help people, but you know they're all just using you. You should be hanging-out with people who can advance your career, not these leeches. I don't get it . . . what's in it for you?"

Feeling somewhat annoyed by his wife's pressure, Jimmy says:

"Debbie, you don't 'get it.' It's really not that hard to figure out. We need cheap actors to fill many roles in our pictures. What better possible place to recruit attractive, ambitious actors than the health club? I'm not getting fleeced. I'm helping our casting people save considerable money on these films. Besides which, I love to work out with young fit people. Trying to look like them keeps me motivated."

Reacting to her husband, Debbie says:

"Jimmy, I don't care who you work out with. That's fine. But when you tell me I can't spend money on new draperies and you're giving them money--that's what gets to me. How does this possibly help me? You know I don't think any of these losers give a damn about you. They're all using you. Don't you remember when you asked Sam to help us move. He told you he had to run to an audition--he didn't lift a finger! Does that sound like anyone who's really a friend? You're dreaming. You should spend more time hanging around people who can really do something for you, not these misfits."

Sensing that she's thinking more about herself, he remarks:

"Debbie, I know you're looking out for me. But doing the draperies has nothing to do with me helping anyone. You remember Michael, don't you? He was another 'zero' I met roller-blading--right? You remember? I got him started with a few non-talking parts. And he was then picked up by our friend Al, who now represents him. You know he's done several features now, don't you? Michael never forgot all the times we had him out to dinner and the pittance I gave him to pay his bills. He never forgot how I helped him when he was down. Did you know that Michael's responsible for my current job? He was working with Jones on another project and brought me up. He called me and set up the meeting and the rest is history."

Jimmy's scenario is not that much different from many others whose personal experience has taught them that doing for others pays off in unexpected ways. Sometimes biting your tongue and not expressing your opinions--even when you're rattled--is the best strategy because you never know when you might need someone's support. Truly, the people you despise the most can turn out to be your best friends. You never really know who's going to help you. Even when you're at the top and feel invincible, it's no assurance that you'll remain on the pedestal. Remaining altruistic is your best assurance that you'll continue successful relating and retain your charisma.

Disguising narcissistic propensities is easier said than done. And without controlling excessive selfishness, charisma will elude your grasp. Many people are so conspicuously selfish and self-absorbed that they're actually unaware when they're serving their own needs. While dealing with their friends, they'll even say things like, "I know this is something *you* really want to do," when, in fact, it's actually something *they* want to do.

Narcissists frequently project their unconscious needs onto others and have difficulty distinguishing what originates inside themselves. When they say, "That person really hates me," narcissists really mean, "I hate them." While asking the mundane question, "Don't you really want Chinese food?," the narcissist is actually saying, "*I* want Chinese food." Well, you get the picture. As long as you're narcissistic it's difficult to acknowledge anyone's needs, other than your own.

A middle-aged political science professor, whose lectures were legendary for nearly intolerable banality, is involved in a tumultuous marriage. His spouse is constantly complaining about his rages and infantile self-centeredness. One day, after running numerous errands for her husband, she returned home failing to bring home his favorite corned beef from a local deli. Flying into a rage the husband says:

"You don't give a damn about me, do you? I ask for so little, and the one thing I do ask you to get me, you don't deliver. I've had it! That's it--I'm out of here. We have irreconcilable personal differences. No matter what you try to do, you just can't make me happy. I know there's got to be a better life somewhere. I'm just not happy in this situation. Somewhere there's got to be some kind of happiness waiting for me."

Stunned by his revelations, the wife says:

"Honey, I think you're really exaggerating our problems. You're going to throw into the wastebasket our 20 year old marriage because of corned beef? That's crazy. How could you be that selfish? We have 3 beautiful boys together. I helped you write and edit your doctoral dissertation. You've completely flipped out. You're going to torpedo our marriage because you didn't get your package of Canter's corned beef? That's completely nuts!"

Having to explain himself further, Jerry says:

"Rhonda, you don't 'get it!' It's not just the corned beef. It's about the fact that we can't agree on anything. We have irreconcilable philosophical differences. C'mon admit it, you really don't like me--do you?"

Not believing what's she's hearing, she reacts:

"Jerry, I feel like I'm in the twilight zone. You're going to destroy our 20 year marriage because I didn't get your corned beef? I can't believe it! What about all the other times you got exactly what you wanted? I've been totally devoted to you. I can't believe you can be so selfish! What about the kids, your family, our friends--what are you going to tell them ? . . . they're going to be completely shocked."

Still showing no signs of coming to his senses, Jerry remarks:

"Rhonda, wake up and smell the coffee--it's over. I'm not going to live the balance of my life in misery. There's got to be a better life and more happiness out there somewhere. I'm not going to be 'guilted' into staying in this thing. It just won't work. Besides, you deserve better! I know there's someone out there who's capable of bringing you some happiness."

Trying to reason with narcissists is a losing battle. Regardless of all the positives, they focus on the negatives which justify their right to engage in irrational behavior, including breaking up a long-term relationship. Jerry's projections on Rhonda are so twisted and based on unresolved past trauma, that he can't see even a glimmer of reality. Thinking in black or white terms, narcissists are incapable of examining ambivalent or mixed emotions and prefer, instead, to adopt extreme, almost indefensible, positions. In Jerry's mind, Rhonda betrayed him by failing-- in this isolated instance--to deliver his corned beef. It sounds crazy, but everything becomes symbolic of all the other accumulated disappointments and failed expectations in their long relationship. Despite missing any real objectivity, the rationale for ending his marriage seems--in the narcissist's mind--legitimate enough.

As we've seen, narcissism paralyzes human relating. No matter how sincerely one wants to relate, showing pathological selfishness introduces major roadblocks to communication--and certainly intimate relating and charisma. Abandoning selfish interest and focusing on serving the needs of others goes a long way in improving relating and charismatic skills. Remaining fixated on yourself guarantees that you'll end up on the 'B' list. By addressing the needs of others you'll soon watch your talents at relating and popularity dramatically improve. When you embrace altruism and sincerely orient yourself around improving the lives of others, your charisma will never be in short supply.

Implacable Faith In Human Potential

Of all the distinguishing features of charisma, none is perhaps more powerful than displaying the unshakable belief in a person's potential. Whether it's a parent having unconditional belief in his child, a teacher showing unwavering faith in her student, or a politician displaying unqualified support for his constituency, the experience of resolute belief in one's potential transcends most obstacles. Charismatic people do more than avoid negativity or prophesies of doom and gloom. They convey an unconditional conviction in an individual's untapped ability.

Regardless of circumstances, when most people have given up, charismatic people have eternal optimism in the potential of striving individuals. Whether someone's lack of accomplishments are attributable to themselves or unfavorable environmental conditions, e.g., poverty and diminished opportunities, the person with charisma shares the unending hope that the struggling individual can achieve his dreams. They keep the dream alive by providing unlimited encouragement when others are singing a chorus of discouragement and negativity.

Promising the hope of a better life--like completing a college degree, finding the right relationship, getting a better job, attaining improved health, acquiring expanded wealth, etc.--irresistibly attracts individuals whose life experience has yielded a ration of disappointment and failure. Expressing instead unbridled enthusiasm for individuals' dreams and potential, charismatic people become instant leaders whose followers show zealous and at times irrational loyalty.

After extracting an individual's self-defeating traits and resurrecting their self-esteem, charismatic people are often idealized and worshipped by their followers. Having ostensibly 'healed' a weakened part to the wannabe's personality, many individuals tend to idolize charismatic people, seldom recognizing their faults, even when they occasionally exploit their vulnerable following. It's a misleading perception of the needy follower that they've been cured or healed, which leads to them to a fantasy-like or delusional sense of well being. The fact that they've identified so strongly with the leader, group, cause or philosophy, temporarily relieves their anxieties and injured self-worth. It's this powerful attachment that leads to potential exploitation.

When feeling 'saved,'--whether it's a wannabe actress, athlete, corporate executive or spiritual disciple--the follower places all their trust and hope in the charismatic leader. The leader's reassurance and validation serves as powerful reinforcement which creates an immediate and automatic sense of well-being. On the other hand, the leader's criticism or condemnation has a comparably powerful but destructive effect, often decimating the follower's self-esteem. Like a parent of a vulnerable child, the charismatic leader is equally in control: They have the power to build up and to tear down. No one should underestimate the power--and responsibility--of this type of charisma and the vulnerability of those seeking all the rewards of coming under the charismatic leader's wing.

A middle-aged married dentist with three children was trapped in a tumultuous marriage for more than 20 years.

For nearly the entire course of his marriage, he couldn't recall a single instance in which he and his spouse weren't attacking each other. With divorce not an option, he was becoming progressively more depressed as his choices seemed to narrow. One day, a close friend invited him to attend an introductory session of a 'growth seminar' which she credits with changing her entire life. She talked glowingly about a young dynamic leader whose energy, wisdom and insight transformed her misery into happiness. Showing considerable skepticism, Bill, the dentist, still decided to take her up on the invitation. What he didn't know at the time was that his friend, Susie, was a recruiter for the seminar, and considered herself a disciple of the leader. Finally deciding to go, Bill anxiously awaited hearing the spiritual guru. At the meeting, the spiritual master welcomed the audience and said:

"Thank you all for joining us. I can assure you that you won't be disappointed. I am well aware that many of you were brought here by former graduates. We're, of course, delighted to have you. But what really brought you here was more than your curiosity. You decided that it's time for a change. Many of you have asked yourself whether you're happy with your current situation . . . and you know the answer. But that's not the whole story either. You're also stuck and don't know what to do. Because it's time for a change, you're here to try to find the path. I can tell you this: If you absorb only 10% of what I have to say, you'll never be the same again. You'll see things in a different light and know what your next step should be. I believe in you 100%! It doesn't matter where you've been and what you've done. The past is the past. Today is your new point of departure. You have it within your power to begin your lives over again. Forget past disappointments, broken promises and painful failures. I believe in your potential and your ability to change. Each of you has the capacity

now as you've had in the past, to do whatever is necessary
to begin your lives over again. Nothing can stop you now,
not even yourself!"

The charismatic leader's presentation sends a powerful
message: He believes in the malcontent's unlimited
potential. As long as he's willing to follow his program,
he's willing to give his unconditional approval. Showing
unconditional acceptance, his non-judgmental position
enables them to make a commitment toward self-
improvement. They're immediately drawn and attracted to
the leader's promises of redemption and offer of utopia.
Despite their backgrounds and history of failure, he's
willing to forgive all their inadequacies and begin anew. It's
the chance to be 'born again'--in a religious context or
otherwise--and the promise of salvation which holds such
irresistible appeal.   Soaking this up, the wannabes and
misanthropes are easily converted and sign over their lives.

Charismatic leaders come in many different packages.
Few are tall, dark and handsome--nor does this really matter;
but all make the same promises. Whether they're addressing
individuals, groups or blocks of voters, their offers of instant
change, redemption and salvation carry a megaton of appeal.
It's the degree of an individual's vulnerability and
desperation that usually determines their susceptibility to
recruitment. Charismatic leaders--regardless of the venue--
possess a keen sense of radar for the vulnerable and needy.
They diagnose and deliver the exact prescription to cure
their followers' defects.   For some it's approval and
encouragement, for others it's a sense of belonging.
Whatever the need, the 'charismatic' leader finds a way of
satisfying it.

When an individual's early life is marked by criticism,
neglect and rejection, they're especially vulnerable to the

tempting offers made by charismatic leaders and other fanatical groups. As good as charismatic leaders are at satisfying these needs, victims of early life neglect are equally vulnerable to these temptations due to their emotional voids. Vulnerable individuals would be well to recognize their weaknesses and proceed with due caution when confronted with charismatic individuals or utopian groups.

While it's easy to become ecstatic or euphoric when someone takes an interest in you, preventing yourself from becoming seduced by tempting but misleading promises is the wisest course. The danger of 'hearing what you believe [due to your own abysmal neediness] and then believing what you hear' [a self-fulfilling prophesy] can be most deceptive. As we've said before, savvy readers would be well advised not to take excessive flattery or validation without some measure of suspicion. Taking things at face value can get you into serious trouble--beware!

Showing implacable faith in another person's potential is a powerful charismatic experience. There's no question that it dramatically improves relating and expands charisma. By exuding enthusiasm, remaining positive and serving as a valued role model, charismatic people have no shortage of friends. Their magic is truly related and proportional to expanding the success of others.

Some Final Thoughts

Relating is a complex interpersonal process which involves much more than basic communication. And without effective relating, developing charisma is a tall order to fill. Although good communication skills are needed for relating, communication alone is no assurance of connecting with people. When communication is combined with a number of *high-level intangibles*, e.g., tact, diplomacy, common sense, good judgment, insight, etc., charismatic relating is made possible. Just as surely, when communication misses high-level intangibles, it remains an empty vehicle for exchanging information, lacking the pizzazz to make things, happen in business or elsewhere.

Charismatic relating is a two-way street requiring reciprocal communication. While it's not necessary to keep the same score, both parties must experience some degree of mutual satisfaction. Narcissistic relating in which one party gets their 'needs' met but the other party is left empty-handed doesn't promote charisma. Remaining consumed with your own needs only blinds you to recognizing how to engage others in mutually satisfying relationships.

Although it's tempting to believe that everyone's a clone of yourself, it's misleading and results in unwarranted disappointment and failure. While *you* might need constant validation and reassurance, that doesn't mean it's the other person's need to give it. In fact, most people whose unconscious habit is usurping others for attention and approval, find themselves short on friends and eventually alienated. It doesn't take too long for most people to runaway for their own survival when they're constantly being ripped-off of their energy.

Transferring high levels of energy to others--not draining them with your own problems--creates the most inviting atmosphere for charismatic relating. Showing a little more healthy co-dependency and less selfishness, is your best guarantee that people won't tire of your company. It's easy and pleasurable to be around people who are lively, non-demanding and giving. Just as certainly, making excessive demands, showing unsightly selfishness and displaying offensive grandiosity is a real turn-off and drives people away.

Recognizing that most people crave recognition, attention and approval goes a long way in diagnosing what needs you must be addressing. Charismatic people tune-in to the needs of others, and do whatever it takes to satisfy them. They're acutely aware that if they accomplish this, they'll possess a powerful measure of influence and create fiercely loyal relationships. Very simply, people are naturally drawn toward individuals who fulfill their needs and avoid individuals who usurp and exploit them. Using validation-- or finding special ways of satisfying important needs--is one of the best paths toward charismatic relating.

It pays to recognize that words do matter. Stating things in conditional and respectful ways opens the doors to otherwise forbidden areas of discussion and communication. Speaking to your audience in comfortable language, using familiar metaphors or examples, also helps to get your message across. Adding credibility by sparingly using creative vocabulary or unforgettable slogans, adds to your measure of influence. Appearing too 'folksy' or pedestrian can backfire by making you appear less intelligent or even patronizing.

Maintaining a good sense of humor shows resiliency and ego-strength. Taking things too literally or seriously detracts from your charisma by creating unwanted defensiveness and unnecessary emotional reactions. Without humor, individuals are less protected and more reactive to life's many disappointments and emotional wounds. Humor keeps things in perspective and provides an extra margin of safety in an otherwise inhospitable environment.

As we've noted, nothing kills charisma faster than narcissism. Showing blatant grandiosity, arrogance and pathological self-centeredness torpedoes successful relating and strips-off charisma. Adopting an altruistic attitude in which you're oriented toward meeting the needs of others seems to help develop charismatic relating. Few people enjoy interacting with pathologically selfish individuals. Remaining self-obsessed practically guarantees that your efforts at relating will fall short of your plans. By addressing the needs of others and expanding their success whenever possible, the path to charisma is more clearly marked.

True relating and charisma involve showing an implacable belief in another person's potential. Encountering someone's resolute belief in your talent, regardless of your background or track-record, is an unforgettable experience driving people toward their personal best. Since most people exposed to negativity are constantly reminded of their inadequacies and failures, encountering a positive force believing in their potential has irresistible appeal. Embracing that inspirational role becomes an unending source of personal charisma.

Points to Remember

- Maintain communication as a two-way street

- Avoid narcissism and self-preoccupation

- Display a high-level of energy and enthusiasm

- Communicate using respectful and conditional language

- Express yourself with creative vocabulary and memorable expressions

- Give attention, recognition and approval whenever possible

- Provide validation and positive social reinforcement

- Display a good sense of humor without sarcasm or insincerity

- Show healthy altruism by orienting yourself toward others

- Remain positive and believe in developing human potential

Chapter *4*

CREDIBILITY
ON THE LINE

In this chapter you'll learn about the many considerations involved in developing and maintaining credibility. Introduction • Image reigns supreme • Lookout for the iceberg Salesmanship is no disgrace • 'Right' doesn't make like • Some final thoughts • Points to remember

Introduction

Credibility and charisma are two sides of the same coin: Without credibility you don't have much charisma and without charisma you don't have much credibility. While charisma can be looked at as the fuel or energy which drives the engines of success, credibility represents the integrity or body of the vehicle. In all interpersonal relations--whether in business or elsewhere--credibility functions like the personality. If the personality is viewed as flawed, factual or not, the bottom falls out of one's credibility.

Many individuals have the propensity to place people on a pedestal, often idealizing qualities and characteristics which don't really exist. For some, the need to idealize is so great and the tendency to evade reality so compelling, that many glaring personality flaws are completely overlooked; they prefer instead, to luxuriate in the painless zone of fantasy land. But when the fantasies are disturbed by 'shocking' revelations, the idealized persons are abruptly dethroned. This rude awakening is usually accompanied by an outpouring of hostility and deprecation of the once worshipped idol or fantasy. So credibility and personality--along with their images of perfection--are fragile commodities that are easily disintegrated.

Related to personality but somewhat distinct is the notion of character. Character is seen as the moral representative of personality: It's the conscience or backbone of the personality structure. In some cases, it's difficult, if not impossible, to find. Character is usually a public perception or inference regarding the ethics of one's deeds. When character is tainted, credibility goes into a free-fall. You can't trust individuals whose personal integrity has been impugned. And without trust, it's difficult to exercise any real measure of charisma, since exerting social influence requires unambiguous impressions of confidence and faith. How can you have faith in people whose images are vitiated by unacceptable and verifiable acts of weakness or vulnerability? You can't. Individuals in whatever type of relationship whose trust has plummeted quickly lose their credibility and charisma.

Sustaining credibility is often a balancing act in which individuals juggle what's practical and expedient against what's ethically 'correct' or morally 'right.' Pragmatics sometimes demand choices which, when viewed retrospectively, can be regretted, especially if they compromise an individual's character. The exigencies of many business or political situations have otherwise ethically-minded persons deviating from their normal routines. It only takes one inadvertent miscue or infraction to damage precious credibility. Like image, it takes a long time to develop, but, with one costly mistake--no matter how accidental--it's gone like the wind.

Apart from questions of integrity, credibility is also sensitive to any unusual changes in routine or status. Even with unequivocal inferences of strong moral integrity, unexpected disappointments or failures can gradually erode precious credibility. Unlike issues of ethical integrity, unwanted disappointments in performance show more latitude in preserving credibility. With a reliable reputation or solid track-record, repetitive failures still take their toll on credibility, eventually depleting it along with its charisma. As usual, reputation can only last so long and take you so far. It's the 'what have you done for me lately' syndrome which still prevails in most circles. A person, for instance, with otherwise solid credibility can watch it take an instant nose dive when simply ousted from their current position of authority. Of course, scrapes with the law or other types of unwanted controversies also drag credibility in the Southern direction.

Maintaining effective interpersonal relating and charisma is less tenable if the individual is *perceived* as flawed in some material or spiritual way. Losing credibility is responsible for more interpersonal and business failures than financial distress. When you're trying to hang on to any position--whether you're a corporate executive, politician, professional athlete or marital partner--credibility is either your best friend or your worst enemy. Capable of bailing you out of many precarious situations, credibility is also known to desert you when you least expect it. When your credibility evaporates, it's difficult to rehabilitate. Most politicians and trial lawyers can attest to this phenomenon. After making publicly humiliating blunders or acutely embarrassing mistakes, the tunnel back appears to have no end in sight. Raising again a familiar case, once credibility heads South, it's difficult to salvage.

A local politician representing a high crime and poverty district, dedicating his career to improving the plight of minorities and the poor, has been arrested for cocaine possession. Caught red-handed by the police using cocaine in his official office, he's publicly humiliated and unable to deny the charges. Asked by the mayor and a number of his colleagues to resign, the elected official remains defiant in his attempt to minimize his problem. At a news conference following his arrest, he's grilled by a feisty reporter:

"Mr. Martinez, can you tell us why you used cocaine on the job? Many of your constituents are especially distressed over the fact you've abused the privilege of your office. It's one thing to have a medical problem requiring treatment, it's still another to use drugs at taxpayers' expense."

Collecting his thoughts and wanting to respond, the elected official remarks:

"Mr. Jones, yes, I'd like to respond very much! First of all, I was depressed due to my mother's death. I was drinking heavily at the time and hung-over so badly in the mornings that I couldn't wake up. I used cocaine to help me overcome these terrible hangovers so I could function on my job. It was the only way of fulfilling my responsibilities to my constituents. I had a job to do and it was the only way I could get my work done."

Sounding incredulous, the reporter takes another swipe at the troubled elected official and says:

"Mr. Martinez, now, if I understand you correctly, you're telling me that you prescribed yourself cocaine to combat disabling hangovers and depression due to your mother's death? Is that correct?"

Apparently believing his own answer, Mr. Martinez remarks:

"Yes, to answer your question, I believe I used cocaine to enable me to perform my duties of elected office. I believe, without the cocaine, I never could have handled my job."

While it's known that credibility is a fragile commodity, Mr. Martinez's answers administer some especially brutal self-inflicted wounds. Certainly his explanation does very little to restore his credibility. In fact, his explanation is so bereft of *plausible deniability*, that he's clearly made matters worse. Although it's too late to categorically deny the reports of cocaine use, offering bewildering explanations only detracts from precious credibility. Not only does he have a credibility problem associated with his arrest for cocaine possession, his own explanations have mortally wounded his efforts at rehabilitation. When faced with a severe credibility crisis, saying or doing things which hurt your cause only digs you into a deeper hole.

When faced with any credibility crisis, rehabilitating credibility is the top priority. As we've said, without credibility, your ability to relate and show charisma are temporarily *disabled*. Restoring charisma, or personal power, involves utilizing important *high-level intangibles*, e.g., timing, tact, diplomacy, 'common sense,' awareness, good judgment and other damage control strategies needed to reverse unfavorable events. Undoing the damage--like repairing fine crystal--is possible, but the repaired version is never quite the same. As in other areas, 'an ounce of prevention is worth a pound of cure.' Although preserving credibility seems like a tall order to fill, it's actually made more manageable by applying the relevant high-level intangibles.

Image Reigns Supreme

Image, like personality, is closely related to credibility:
It's a public or external perception based on observable
behavior. It doesn't really reflect the true essence of the
person but instead is a cosmetic--although indispensable--
impression. Acting consistently over time (even if it's
consistently inconsistent) usually takes care of creating an
image--good, bad or indifferent. Images are, in effect,
superficial perceptions that stereotype an individual's
personality and behavior. What you see isn't necessarily
what you get, but it's all that others can be expected to
experience. A person's image--like the one they see in the
mirror--is a reflection of the way other people see them. If,
instead, it's a reflection only of the way they see themselves,
then the person's probably headed for trouble.

It really doesn't matter how individuals see themselves.
What counts is how others view them. Problems arise when
there's a big gap between how you see yourself and how
others experience you. You may see yourself as a
'wonderful' person, but if others perceive you as obnoxious
or offensive, then that's your image. It matters, of course,
how a person feels inside, but when it comes to image, it's
only experienced by others externally. Proclaiming, "that's
not really me," doesn't ignore the fact that what others see
has the final say. Without discounting what's truly inside a
person, if the image projected reflects a dramatically
different view from how they see themselves, then the
person's awareness and insight are poor. Awareness and
insight are important high-level intangibles responsible for
effective communication and protecting credibility and
charisma.

Since charisma involves personal power and since
credibility reflects a person's integrity, cultivating a positive
image is crucial for success. Showing poor awareness and
insight blinds individuals to how they impact their audience

and hurt their credibility. Once again, credibility represents the structure or integrity of the individual. Without it, charisma is an unstable essence difficult to capture and impossible to use. Possessing awareness alerts you to how you're affecting others and controlling your image. Generally speaking, most people try to cultivate an image of confidence and integrity. Appearing anxious and untrustworthy hurts credibility and dissolves charisma: Confidence is king!

Image is affected by many factors including physical appearance, body language, eye-contact, speech, tone of voice, mood or any other factor causing a change in perception. Raising or lowering your voice, redirecting your eye-contact, vacillating in your moods, expressing yourself crudely, ventilating your emotions or folding your arms on your chest, all transmit different messages. Transforming yourself from cool and collected to hostile and unstable telegraphs very different signals to your audience. Credibility and image are noticeably altered when you're unaware of mood swings and noticeable changes in body language.

Awareness is key because it's your best tool for maintaining control. Let's face it, if you're out-of-control--emotionally or otherwise--it's going to be tough to uphold a favorable image. And if your image goes, you can readily expect your relating skills and charisma to follow close behind. Reactivity--or the tendency toward impulsive, knee-jerk responses--is a sure sign that your image is taking a serious hit. Protecting your image requires planning, calculation and careful execution. Constant emotional over-reactions are bound to derail you from completing your goals in business or social relationships. When predictable over-reactions occur, it's a sure sign that a person is either under unmanageable stress or has unmistakable personality defects, e.g., a lack of impulse control.

A professional basketball player, known for his flamboyance on and off the court, is advised by his publicist to clean up his act. After a series of impulsive episodes, his image headed south along with several commercial endorsements. Following his agent's advice, he's made a special effort to stay in control, including going to a sports psychologist to improve his aggressive and self-defeating tendencies. Going along with his publicist's program, he even participated in a fund-raiser for under-privileged youths. His image seemed to be on its way up. Raising his publicist's blood pressure, he attacked a photographer and kicked him in the groin during a recent game. Toweling off in the locker room after his ejection, he's approached by an inquisitive reporter who asks:

"Mr. Staffman, we thought you'd changed your image. You were even going to a sports psychologist. What happened to you? We had heard reports that Nike was considering taking you back--but, now, after this incident, they'd be nuts. What would you like to tell your fans?"

With his blood boiling and ready to pounce on the reporter, the basketball player says:

"How dare you track me down into my locker room. You guys don't know when to quit! That photographer said something that pissed me off. You know what--he got exactly what he deserved. I ain't no pussy. As far as my fans are concerned, they know who I really am. I don't have to be explaining myself. They know that I'm a good person. Everyone knows that he provoked me--what a jerk! Maybe, next time they'll think twice before messing with me."

Incredulous of Staffman's total lack of contrition, the reporter continues his line of questioning:

"Look Jimmy, you're the one with the image problem--not me. I'm not the one trying to control myself. Aren't you going to take any responsibility for the incident? League officials have a right to know whether you're even safe to put back on the court. I've heard you're going to be booked for assault and battery. What's it going to take before you finally 'get it?' I'm going to give you another chance to publicly state your position. OK, what is it?"

Looking defiant as ever, the basketball player remarks:

"I've got no reason to apologize. You guys have had it in for me from day one. You're the ones who pushed me to do it. It makes a great story! Just imagine what it'd be like to report only on boring basketball stats? You've all made me what I am. I'm a mirror of how bored everyone is. Don't blame me for acting out now and then. I just like to keep everyone awake. You guys love it! What the hell would you do without me?"

Rehabilitating a fallen image in more easily said than done. Image takes years to develop and an instant to destroy. As unsightly as Staffman's behavior was on the court, his off the court responses to the reporter were equally offensive. His unbridled grandiosity and wholesale lack of contrition have done very little to resurrect his fallen image. In fact, his arrogance, conceit and noticeable paranoia have left the fans and press flat-out disgusted with his antics. Expecting commercial sponsors to jump back on the bandwagon, is more than unrealistic--it's almost delusional. Showing callous insensitivity to others does very little to get beyond a credibility crisis. In fact, it just makes a bad situation worse.

Salvaging credibility requires more than following special damage control strategies--although, if followed to the letter, they do help. Attempting to rehabilitate reputation and credibility by attending phony fund-raisers or staged photo-ops, doesn't help when one's personality continues to run out-of-control. Displaying inflated narcissism, with its revolting public exhibitions, invites a host of unsympathetic reactions including possible reprisals. How can you talk about rehabilitating a sullied image when your own impulsive actions make matters worse? Clearly, the first step toward image recovery is demonstrating self-control. The next step involves incorporating invaluable high-level intangibles your responses. Words really do matter.

Had basketball player Staffman shown more class, he would have elicited a very different reaction from the reporter. Demonstrating better control over his narcissistic propensities and incorporating some *high-level intangibles*, Staffman could have said:

"First, let me just say that I deeply regret my loss of control. I've been working hard with my sports psychologist on learning better control. Like substance abusers, we all have a tendency to backslide. I want to personally apologize to the photographer for my loss of control. There's absolutely no excuse for that kind of behavior. I fully intend to make it up to him in any way that I can. As for my fans, I just want them to know how I sorry I am for disappointing them. I can't tell them how much I appreciate their continued support. I'm especially grateful to the press for allowing me to share my real feelings."

Nothing moves beyond a credibility crisis more than showing sincere contrition. Given that you can't reverse what you've done and that making *categorical denials* would exacerbate the situation, offering a sincere apology has almost magical healing properties. Showing empathy and using validation also helps make a bad situation better, Trying to turn an unforgivable situation inside-out by blowing smoke and using mega-doses of spin can backfire. While there's certainly a time and place for using spin, sometimes engaging in too much implausible explanation can get you into more hot water. With poorly timed and farfetched explanations, you can inadvertently jump from a frying pan into a fire.

A popular comedian and actor is arrested and booked in the wee hours of the morning for soliciting a prostitute. He's found with the prostitute (with an arrest record a mile long) driving in his 500 SL Mercedes heading east bound on Sunset Boulevard. Within hours, the media are alerted to this major news event, as he's due to be released on bail. Sending his publicist into gyrations, his coterie of handlers are left scrambling for a plausible explanation. Faced with potentially ruining his image, he reluctantly faces the press and responds to an avalanche of questions. A reporter from one of the well known show-biz trade publications asks:

"Mr. Mosby, what were you doing with a prostitute in your car on Sunday morning? It seems obvious to most people, but we're hoping you've got a better excuse. Can you tell us what you were doing at that hour giving her a ride?"

Up to the task, the comedian remains collected and says:

"Actually, it's really quite simple. With all the pressure, I've been suffering from terrible insomnia lately. It was a warm night and I just decided to take a leisurely drive down Sunset Boulevard. While cruising down the Boulevard, I spotted this poor young women who seemed lost and needed a ride. I was concerned about her, so I picked her up to give

her a lift home. Hey, it's a jungle out there that late . . . and
I was only trying to help her out--that's what happened. I
know the police are looking for a more titillating story, but
unfortunately, that's the boring truth."

On the surface, this seems like a fairly reasonable
explanation, at least to those without a jaundiced eye. It has
all the trappings of an innocent, altruistic gesture, despite
the fact that he supplies rather incredulous details, including
his apparent 'insomnia' prompting his midnight 'joy-ride.'
Suggesting that he was giving a well known prostitute a lift
home at 3:00 AM lacks *plausible deniability*, leading law
enforcement authorities to doubt his explanation. In order to
meet the standard of plausible deniability, the explanation
must fit some reasonable range of believability. Whether
his excuse fits that range is ultimately measured by how
many people buy his explanation.

When faced with criminal charges, most defendants--or
criminal defense attorneys--offer exculpatory explanations
ranging in plausible deniability from the conservative and
reasonable to the radical and farfetched. Usually, if it's
possible, the shorter the stretch, the better the credibility.
The more twists and turns on explanations, usually the more
problems with plausibility. But sometimes the luxury of
conservative explanations aren't possible and more
incredulous descriptions have to be offered. In the end,
regardless of the explanation, image has a lot to do with
what's found credible.

When the crime doesn't fit the image or the image doesn't
fit the crime--despite all the evidence to the contrary--then
even tenuous alternative explanations can suffice. In the
case above, because the celebrity had no prior arrest records
and because he's viewed as a somewhat likable individual,
his spin seemed to work. Had he had prior arrests for

solicitation or other nefarious activities, his image might not have saved him. On the other hand, had his image been thoroughly wasted, and had his jaunt down Sunset Boulevard really been purely innocent and accidental, his story would have been totally discredited. Having an impeccable image usually secures individuals the benefit of the doubt--regardless of the situation. But the opposite is also true. Obviously, it's certainly preferred to have a squeaky-clean image.

In most legal proceedings--criminal or otherwise--it's the objective of opposing counsel to discredit the opposition's image. Finding some aspect of inconsistency--no matter how minute or 'immaterial'--can have an impact of impeaching one's image. The fact that something seems immaterial doesn't mean that it's irrelevant. What's relevant is the process of finding anything that chips away at image and credibility--whether it's gossip or innuendo, tabloid reports, prior arrests, third-party accounts or any other sources of indictable information. That's the name of the game.

Recent high-profile criminal trials involving celebrities attest to the fact that image serves as a protective membrane, shielding suspects from otherwise incontrovertible evidence. If nothing else, observers of these proceedings know that any evidence--no matter how persuasive or damaging--is impeachable. Contrary to what you may think, facts don't speak for themselves; attorneys and witnesses speak for the facts. Many have questioned whether celebrities--because of their carefully honed images--are even capable of receiving impartial trials. When so much is already known about a person or their particular crimes, how is it possible to select juries with sufficient impartiality? What's enough impartiality is anyone's guess. But certainly with high-profile celebrity trials, image can be a distracting smoke screen.

Image, credibility and charisma are closely tied together because most people really do judge a book by its cover. What you see is usually what you get. Mind-reading or speculating about a person's true intentions, rarely changes external perceptions. Maintaining a healthy facade or image helps protect people from unexpected daily hits on their credibility. As we've said, when your image is tainted, so too is your credibility and ultimately your charisma. Preserving image is a vigilant process requiring careful attention and monitoring. Unconscious lapses, in which unresolved conflicts and 'unfinished business' surface in unwanted and unpredictable ways, can't be ignored. Developing improved awareness and insight pays many unexpected benefits.

Lookout for the Iceberg

Hanging onto credibility--like your bank account--is very much related to staying in control of your life. If you're derailed riding a variety of tangents, bingeing on food, sex, gambling, excessive entertainment or any other obsession, you'll find your credibility slipping to new lows. As long as you're driven by forces beneath your awareness, you can't stay in charge of most business and social situations. While this probably makes sense, unconscious forces aren't logical--they're *psychological.* They operate independently of your good judgment and 'common sense' and have a mind of their own. Realistically, it's impossible to plot out any coherent path in business or everyday life when your unconscious is calling the shots.

Although there are no guarantees, getting-in-touch with your 'darker' side affords a better measure of control. This is easier said than done, since many people literally spend a fortune in psychoanalysis trying to get a handle on this problem. Why deny something exists when it winds up costing you dearly? For many people, it's the path of least resistance. It's easier to push away the pain and bad memories. While it creates discomfort to examine hidden parts of yourself, it's also your best protection that you won't wind up shooting yourself in the foot--self-destructing.

Staying on the course of success requires methodical planning, strategizing and pursuing targeted goals. It's difficult to maintain any meaningful direction if you're sidetracked by unconsciously-driven distractions. While there's nothing wrong with pleasure, it's still another thing to be bingeing out-of-control or, perhaps even worse, is thinking that you're firmly in charge of yourself or your life, when in fact you're on the verge of spontaneously self-destructing. Most people, whose lifestyles weren't inherited or handed to them on a silver platter and whose efforts toward their goals cost them dearly, simply can't afford to blow it when they're striving for the top.

Looking out for the iceberg involves paying closer attention to unconscious processes. Ignoring them, like traffic signals, can lead to unwanted calamities. Making the *unconscious conscious*, or creating self-awareness, is a major goal of psychoanalysis and most psychotherapies. With self-awareness comes the internal control and protection that struggling to attain your goals won't cause you to crash and burn at your own hands. Tuning-in to that little internal voice which says, in effect, 'listen to me and let me be your guide,' starts a dialogue between the tip and bottom of the iceberg.

Linking the conscious and unconscious parts of personality or making the unconscious conscious, automatically creates more internal control. It's actually a simple--but not easy--process of focusing your attention on what you're feeling at a given moment. Once you know what you're feeling, then you can begin to trace the emotion to its source. The fact that something is held repressed in the unconscious gives it power: It's like a tempest in a tea pot. Regardless of how inconsequential the original event, once it's repressed it appears to gain its own power and momentum. After you confront it, it quickly loses its steam--and almost appears like it wasn't even real.

Let's say, for instance, a person is tuned-in to their fear of public speaking. The first step involves identifying the fear and next tracing it to its historical root. It might have been due to a negative event at school or in their family. Suppose they remember an event in which they were criticized by their teacher while making an oral report. At that point, they ask themselves, "What am I feeling?," to which they identify experiencing, let's say, hurt and anger. After acknowledging that it's OK to have these feelings, they express and release any pent-up emotion. The grip of its traumatic effect begins to loosen.

After the emotions connected with the historical event are acknowledged and expressed, the anxiety experienced in current time over 'public speaking' seems to lose it's kick. The unconscious is now conscious, and realizing that the source of their fear stems from a childhood mishap which has no relevancy today, the traumatic event is now released from the unconscious. What's surprising is the fact that once the repressed emotion is turned loose, it loses all its force. Something which previously created heart palpitations and sweating, now has virtually no effect at all. Although this process seems easy to some, others find the help of a therapist a welcomed relief. The bottom line is that it doesn't really matter *how* this problem is dealt with, but rather *whether* it's eventually resolved.

While attempting to preserve credibility and charisma, it's essential that self-destructive propensities are neutralized. By having improved control over unconscious dynamics, individuals are assured that career and social mishaps are related to factors truly beyond their control. It just isn't acceptable to fail or sabotage success because your *unconscious* decides that it's your time to take a fall.

A well known baseball executive, whose career in front office management spanned over 40 years and whose humble beginnings in the depression made his accomplishments all the more remarkable, was regarded at the top of his trade. Frequently consulted by other baseball executives, his knowledge of the game was considered gifted and unsurpassed. Although considering himself a private person, he still relished the limelight and all the attention earned from his accomplishments. Interviewed frequently by various electronic and print media, he considered his relationship with the press second nature. On the 50th anniversary of Jackie Robinson's historic entrance into the major leagues, he's interviewed via satellite-feed on a nationally syndicated news program. The interviewer, a seasoned TV news anchor, considered one of the most decorated figures at the top of his field, asks:

"Mr. McMannis, 50 years after breaking the 'color' barrier in major league baseball, could you tell us your thoughts on this historic occasion about the role of Blacks in front office or executive management positions?"

Showing no hesitation about the question, the executive remarks:

"I believe there's been great progress from the days in which I grew up and this country didn't even know it had a racial problem. You see Mr. Frankel, Blacks were raised by plantation owners to be bigger and brawnier than Whites. They're stronger, faster and more durable athletes than Whites. As for front office jobs, I'm not sure that they really have what it takes to succeed."

After hearing in disbelief his 'politically incorrect'--even disastrous--comments on live national television, the TV anchor presses on for clarification:

"I guess what you mean is the fact that they've never been given the opportunity to perform in upper management positions. Given the chance, what do you think of their future opportunities to succeed in upper management of major league baseball?"

Following the same line of reasoning, the baseball executive remarks:

"I think it's possible, but you have to acknowledge where their skills and talents are best utilized. 'They' make good base or batting coaches since they've had that experience. I just happen to think they're best utilized in positions in which they have proven talents."

Falling hard on the heels of the interview [within 24 hours] the 'organization' euphemistically announces Mr. McMannis' abrupt 'resignation,' more realistically, his summary dismissal. Forty years of hard-earned expertise and accolades crashed and burned in a matter of minutes, without any chance of salvation. His baseball career had ended in a flash. All the deals, the trades, the difficult negotiations, the championship teams, and, yes, the many long-standing relationships and 'loyal' friendships, vaporized that quickly. Although the present discussion isn't focused on the executive's diplomatic failures or learning the exigencies of *political correctness*, he clearly made what amounted to a fatal miscalculation.

While it's easy to dismiss this costly blunder as accidental, it's more fruitful to examine how and why it occurred. Although it could be argued that interviews via satellite-feed lull people into a false sense of security, the fact that someone has years of media savvy certainly goes against that theory. More realistically accounting for this irreversible lapse, were probably unconscious wishes to sabotage his career. Perhaps due to guilt, possibly unworthiness or low self-esteem, or maybe a just a desire to take an early retirement, statements were made which torpedoed his success. All his previous credibility and charisma were suddenly evaporated into thin air.

Powerful unconscious factors stemming from many different causes--if left unchecked--can come back to bite you if you ignore their existence. Tuning-in to your feelings and tracing the emotion back to its roots helps expose potential trip-wires to success. With so much riding on every deal, most people can't allow the mass of the iceberg to remain submerged. Recognizing the unconscious parts of personality is good preventive medicine, especially because most people don't want to be their own worst enemies.

Choosing awareness over a more benighted state automatically improves control over most situations-- although gaining insight is no piece of cake. When unconscious factors take charge of the personality, it's difficult to maintain credibility because the person never really gets honest feedback about their behavior. As long as someone blames others for their weaknesses and failures, it's difficult to develop the personal awareness of the role they're playing in their own problems. Falsely attributing all your failures to *others* but all your successes to *yourself*, prevents you from accepting personal responsibility and participating in your own destiny.

Blaming others or projecting your own repressed shortcomings, assures that awareness and internal control won't come easily. In fact, blaming others guarantees that helpful emotional insights will remain buried and unusable. Many fragile personalities, whose narcissistic propensities leave them too defensive to receive constructive feedback and whose haughtiness and arrogance prevents them from learning valuable lessons, project their unacceptable weaknesses onto others. Without owning these shameful or embarrassing parts of themselves, they find continuous faults with individuals or groups with whom they're involved.

When repressed trauma exists, perhaps stemming from early-life abuse or neglect, individuals can sometimes fabricate false memories to further shield the personality from facing the 'truth.' False memories--or distorted recollections--serve the useful purpose of temporarily avoiding pain but actually assure that individuals will have long-term problems in relationships and elsewhere. False memories take people off the path of self-awareness and onto a collision course with chronic unhappiness. Since many early-life memories are real, determining which ones are manufactured is a piece of work.

A 40 year old litigator, whose flamboyant personality flashed like a neon sign and whose prospects of settling down seemed progressively dismal, always blamed her failures on 'bad luck.' She couldn't, for the life of her, figure out why most men didn't call her back after the first

date. Having striking looks and a commanding personality,
she often wondered what she was doing wrong. Joining a
video dating service, she rarely found herself short of dates.
The introductions were always stimulating, but the dates
seem to eventually fizzle out. Watching most of her friends
eventually get married, she was growing more exasperated
and hopeless. While at lunch with a gay friend in whom she
frequently confided, she asks:

"Alex, what gives? I don't have a clue what I'm doing
wrong. We always have a lot of fun--don't we? You've
really got to be up-front with me. Why doesn't anyone ever
call me back after the first date? Do I really look that bad?
Am I such a terrible person? I just can't figure it out.
You've got to help me. Please, be honest. I really need to
know what you think!"

Hearing her frustration and wanting to respond but not
wanting to come off too strong, her friend Alex says:

"Kristi, you're fabulous! I love getting together with you.
You've got a great sense of humor. You make me crack up
all the time. And, if that's not enough, you're so intelligent
and attractive. Girl, you're really sexy. It's hard to know
what's wrong with these guys. They just have to accept you
for who you are. I mean . . .well . . . you're really dynamic.
There's nothing you don't know. You're up on everything.
Most of these guys are probably blown away when they're
around an intelligent woman."

Still not getting it, Kristi goes on and comments:

"Look Alex, I appreciate all your kind words. But let's
face, it doesn't do me any good. There's something about
me that guys just don't like. I really need to know what it is.
I'm running out of time--life is passing me by. You were

saying, I'm dynamic, intelligent . . . and there's nothing I
don't know. Maybe I'm too opinionated and competitive--I
always have to be right."

Showing the first signs of possible awareness, Alex feels a
little more at liberty to cut to the chase and says:

"Kristi . . . don't get me wrong, but maybe you're a little
too ballsy. Most guys need all the stroking they can get.
And if you're too busy getting all the strokes for yourself,
maybe you're not paying enough attention to them. When
you're out on a date, maybe you get nervous or something. I
know that if you acted the way you do with me, you
wouldn't have any problems. You're funny, charming,
sexy, entertaining . . . you've got it! One thing that comes to
mind: How did you get along with your father?"

Coming out of left field and surprised that he'd bring that
up, Kristi responds:

"Alex, you're really amazing. All these years we've
known each other and you've never brought him up.
Actually, even more surprising, is the fact that I've never
brought him up. Well, if you really want to know . . . my
parents divorced when I was 3 years of age. I was the
youngest child and I always felt I had to compete for my
father's attention. I mean--I had to get the best grades and
always have the answers. I mean, I had to be perfect . . .
better than my brothers and sister. I think when I'm around
a strong male, I get very competitive. I never let them get a
word out, before interrupting them with the answers."

Sensing less defensiveness and more openness than usual,
Alex goes on:

"You know Kristi . . . I think you're onto something. Maybe you have a lot of unresolved anger when dealing with men, especially those who, on some level, remind you of your father. It couldn't have been too pleasant as a child to constantly have to jump through all his hoops. His love seemed so conditional on you being perfect. Maybe you've held over a resentment which comes out in disguised ways when you're out on dates with strong men. It's just a thought. But it might account for why you've had so many problems."

Looking like the cat who just swallowed the canary, Kristi remarks:

"Alex, I think you're definitely onto something. I can be with you and be totally comfortable. But other men bring out something in me. I become so nervous--and I guess hostile. I never realized I was carrying around so much resentment toward my father."

Kristi's case isn't that different from many others whose unconscious hostility or fear prevent them from developing satisfactory relationships. It just happened that Kristi's unresolved resentment toward her father led her to express it in disguised ways toward men with whom she got involved. Regardless of all her charisma and 'dynamic' personality, she quickly turned off her dates by monopolizing conversations and appearing too competitive. Her credibility and charisma suffered by allowing unidentified hostility to filter through in all her interactions with prospective boyfriends. Her lack of awareness sabotaged her best efforts at developing a satisfying love relationship.

Although Kristi thought she was in control of most situations, the truth was that the bulk of her iceberg was calling the shots. Her unconscious resentment stored from childhood, managed--despite all her best efforts--to undermine her overtures at relating to the opposite sex. This intelligent, funny, dynamic and entertaining person was usurped of her charisma by unwanted baggage from her childhood. Once recognizing the sources of her feelings, Kristi was better able to contain her negative feelings and express them in more constructive ways. Rather than projecting them on her dates, she was able to deal with them on more realistic terms. It's not that she got along with everyone, but at least she no longer used them as a punching bag to unload her own unconscious anger. Without the chip on her shoulder, she was able to allow the best side of her personality to come out.

Just as Kristi found herself over-reacting in many social situations, many others find themselves in the same boat. As long as you're reactive without *real* provocation, it's difficult to orchestrate your agenda in a methodical way. How do you maintain credibility and charisma, when you're acting like a loose canon? Carrying around unfinished business is one of the surest ways to self-destruct when you least expect it. Paying closer attention to your feelings, tracing emotions to their historical roots and expressing pent-up feelings in appropriate ways, helps assure that your 'darker' side doesn't wind up defeating you.

Salesmanship Is No Disgrace

There's a paradoxical view about salesmanship: On the one hand it's viewed as distasteful, while on the other hand, it's seen as highly admirable. Many people are ashamed of selling themselves, preferring instead to defer this unenviable task to their designated agents. Boasting about someone's abilities is OK for their spouses, agents, parents, managers or friends, but it's considered the height of grandiosity to engage in too much self-promotion. Despite this fact, failing to self-promote is one of the biggest downfalls to success for many people. Individuals' reluctance to blow their own horn stems at least partly from the notion that it's considered offensive to comment too loudly about yourself. There's a fine line between confidence and conceit. And ironically, self-deprecation is far more acceptable than making self-congratulatory remarks.

When walking on the razor's edge, between healthy self-regard and conceit, it's important to promote your own talents without sounding grandiose or haughty. Without some measure of self-confidence, attaining your personal goals can be an uphill battle. Developing credibility and charisma is, to a large extent, a function of self-promotion. Expecting others to promote your ideas or personal talents can be a long wait. Perceptions of credibility are related to how you present and promote yourself. If you see yourself as too tentative and weak, you can expect others to see you in the same light.

Believing in yourself and overcoming fears of rejection, is often a major step on the path to establishing credibility. It's difficult to talk about personal credibility if you're your own worst critic. While it's tempting--and even charming--to engage in humorous self-deprecation, it's also self-defeating when you're promoting negative perceptions. Speaking well of yourself is preferred to engaging in too much self-ridicule or condemnation. It's difficult to promote an image of credibility when you're facetiously running yourself down. You may 'get' the levity, but others can easily miss your intent. Striking a balance between showing tasteful humor, itemizing your attributes and avoiding excessive grandiosity is a difficult balancing act. But it's one that must be performed.

Selling yourself is a delicate blend between presenting your best qualities and, at the same time, showing a human side. Talking yourself up too much risks creating impressions of conceit and grandiosity, stripping away precious credibility and charisma. Allowing people to *observe* your best side is preferred over directly ringing your bell. When others see you at your best, in whatever capacity, it speaks louder than your own words. Hard selling people on your many talents and gifts usually boomerangs, often creating suspicion when it shouldn't even exist. A 'softer' sell in which you permit others to draw their own conclusions about your talents by observing your charm, intelligence, articulation, and presentation carries the most weight.

Showing sensitivity and consideration goes a long way in creating a positive impression and credibility. When you're directing your undivided attention and energy toward others and restraining your own narcissistic agenda--whether for approval or any other reason--your self-promotion skills will increase many fold. Disguising your own agenda and orienting yourself around satisfying the needs of others, is your best style of self-promotion. Only then will your audience remain receptive to hearing and seeing your many talents. It's clearly paradoxical that the harder you try to sell yourself, the less convincing your pitch. The more aloof or less invested you seem, the more credibility you'll establish.

An ambitious wannabe screenwriter, whose prior scripts have come 'close but no cigar' but whose love of writing won't be deterred, gets a call from his agent setting up a meeting with the president of production for a low budget, but prestigious film studio. He's ecstatic about getting the chance to pitch his most recent project--a romantic comedy about infiltration and subversion in the fashion industry.

Expressing considerable anxiety about the upcoming meeting, his agent tries to brief him on what to expect. During a tele-conference, his agent says:

"Michael, this is definitely the furthest we've gotten on one of your projects to date. The good news is, we're finally in the door . . . the bad news is it's a long way from being a done deal. But that's OK. We're getting a chance to pitch the project. That's all you can expect. We can also assume that it's already gone through a preliminary screening. It's been reviewed and now we're going on to the next level. Does that make sense?"

Feeling quite excited about the prospects of pitching the project, the writer says:

"Lauren, you've done a great job just getting us to this point. Believe me, I'm well aware that this is a long way from over. But I can't help from feeling ecstatic that someone liked it enough to invite us to a meeting. As the writer, I'm really not sure what I should say. Obviously, I like my own work. Do you think I should try to sell them on the script or should I act sort of indifferent? What do think the best strategy might be? You know I have a tendency to under-sell myself--even put myself down. I always prefer to let you talk-up my work. How do you think I should handle the meeting?"

Getting a sense that Michael needs some direction, Lauren remarks:

"Michael, it's really important that you're not overly self-deprecating in the meeting. You've got a great acerbic sense of humor. But others might take it the wrong way. I mean, I want you to be yourself, but I've noticed, over the years, your tendency to disparage your own writing. I think, obviously, you need to be natural--to a point--but you also need to show some energy and enthusiasm for your project. You get the picture?"

Sometime later at the pitch meeting, the president of production puts the writer in the hot seat and says:

"Michael . . . glad you could join us today. My script reviewer really likes your piece. Give me the 'high concept.'"

Trying to restrain a barely audible gulp, the screenwriter tries to collect himself and says:

"The movie is about, intrigue, nudity, lingerie, infiltration, subversion and corporate politics in the fashion industry. It's about envy, jealousy, competition, market share and the steamy interpersonal relationships in which deals are made."

Responding to his description, the president of production remarks:

"OK . . . That's good! I like that. What's different about this from other treatments of the fashion or modeling industry recently made into movies? Who's the audience? Why should we make this film?"

Demonstrating some added persuasion, the writer responds:

"First of all, I think I've written a better screenplay than anything else out there. No one has even come close to describing the inside dynamics of the fashion industry. Remember, I used to be a designer myself and know all the players. You can probably tell by reading it, that there's a high level of psychological accuracy to the characters. I've tried to capture the manipulation, gamesmanship, quid pro quo's and sex, all of which I lived through when I worked in the industry. The characters were literally right out of the people I worked with on a daily basis. If you're interested in portraying the industry, you've chosen the right screenplay. But you're going to need to move quickly on the project. I've got several other studios interested in the script . . . and it's going to go to whoever places the first offer. If the offers all come in at once, I can't control a competitive bid situation. I hope you're interested."

On closer inspection of the dialogue, Michael needed all the coaching he could get. Although he tried to follow his agent's advice and avoid too much self-deprecation, he might have gone overboard in the opposite direction. Monopolizing the conversation and blowing his horn too loudly doesn't put his best foot forward. Showing too much bravado and grandiosity doesn't engender confidence, it creates unwanted suspicion and distrust. While it's one thing to show self-confidence, it's still another to be derisive toward the works of others and overly self-congratulatory.

Attempting, as Michael did, to back the hearse up to the door only left the studio chief more defensive and leery of the project. His hard-sell might have sealed his fate by reducing his credibility and turning off the savvy production executive. Pushing too hard--regardless of the commodity--creates an impression of quiet desperation, leading to a devaluation of the 'stock,' and, in this case, the script. Taking another tact, a softer-sell in which you reel in your narcissistic enthusiasm--just a bit--and feign *mild* indifference might have upped the executive's interest in the project. As it was, if something has to be pushed with so much pressure, it usually creates lowered interest. Armed with this new approach, the writer recalculates his strategy and says:

"Mr. Goldenberg, it's good to be here . . . and, by the way, I thought your last film was a classic. Now, the 'high concept' is simple: The script's about, envy, greed, intrigue, corporate espionage, lingerie, nudity and the lurid interpersonal relationships in the fashion industry. It might not be right for your studio, and we're not quite sure where it will end up. I hope you find it appealing."

While considerably more laconic, Michael's new response introduces some subtle elements. A little stroking always sets things on the right track. After all, although you're in need of reassurance, other people--even in high places--also like receiving approval and validation. While the 'high concept' is fairly straightforward, the disguised reverse psychology adds to the project's appeal and attractiveness. Hinting that he doesn't really know where the script will end up, invites greater temptation since the executive certainly wouldn't want it to fall into the hands of one of his competitors. Showing less pushiness and giving more space, automatically creates more credibility and greater interest in the project, regardless of the venue.

Soft-selling shouldn't be confused with passivity and a failure of nerve on the part of various promoters. At the same time, knowing when it's time to back off the throttle is also part of timing and finesse. As with most extremes-- whether it's too much aggression or passivity--neither polarity is an effective tactic. We all know that there's a fine line between pushiness and persistence, but good salespeople know when it's right to press forward with their case. Whether they're cognizant of what they're doing, they engage in strategic planning and calculation. Winging it and flying by the seat of your pants, works for the very lucky 'intuitive' types but not the vast majority.

When your counterpart [the buyer] is expressing their opinion, it's not the time to express yours. Showing restraint at the right times, is part of learning the *high-level intangibles* of timing and tact. The opening usually comes when you see a change in their body language and speech. When 'buyers' sit back, finish talking and open their eyes and mouths, it's time to make your pitch. Obviously, interrupting this sequence risks alienating your most important audience. Paying closer attention to tact and timing, savvy promoters pick their moments in which to pounce on opportunities.

Calling it quits too soon is one of the biggest stumbling blocks to many promotion-minded individuals. Fearing rejection, salespeople often procrastinate making presentations when they should be staying in touch. And yet counterbalancing, when it's time to back off and allow the 'account' an opportunity to assimilate 'the offer,' is also a tough call. Salespersons' should neither be unduly passive nor overly aggressive, but appropriately sensitive to the window of opportunity. When the window opens, you have to know when to climb through. At the same time, you also have to know when to back off and call it a day. When the buyer's receptivity seems low, give them time to assimilate your proposal. Becoming fixated on a project and pushing too hard is usually counterproductive.

Overcoming objections is one of the most difficult challenges in any sales-oriented business. Without mastering this skill, there's little room for developing credibility or charisma. If the door is slammed in your face too often, you're not going to be closing too many deals. Fanning the flames of most deals involves maintaining conversations even when you feel like breaking them off. You never know exactly when you're going to close a deal, but you can rest assured that you won't have any deal if you fail to communicate effectively. It's better to communicate and fail then to fail to communicate.

Making commitments is difficult for most people. Whether it's in relationships or business transactions, the same fears paralyze people from making decisions--no matter how trivial or important. Many people think, 'what if I'm making the wrong decision,' and, rather than jumping in, they equivocate and put decisions--even simple ones--on hold. By listening attentively, showing empathy and acknowledging the buyer's right to equivocate, otherwise impossible looking obstacles can be circumvented. While dealing with objections, it's important to note that fear plays a major role. When you help people deal with their anxieties, previous objections seem to pale into insignificance.

A new car salesman, whose aggressive style was touted by his manager as an ideal role-model for other salespersons and yet whose closing-ratio lagged far behind expectations, never hesitates to show his bravado to prospective buyers. Boasting of his unmatched knowledge of his vehicles and his influence over his sales manager, he was known to usurp other salespersons of their customers. While interacting with customers he showed little patience especially with ambivalent buyers. Trying to muscle his way with an ambivalent customer, he engages in his typical hard-sell and says:

"Bill, what's holding you back? It's the money, isn't it? Stop worrying about whether you can afford the vehicle. Everyone gets cold feet before making a big purchase. Just think of it this way: You're young and will continue to increase your salary over the next several years . . . I mean you're the type who's really going somewhere. You'll see, this car will really help your career. You're not afraid that you're heading for a demotion are you? In all likelihood, you're going to be making more money in the future. So, stretching yourself a little now for the more expensive model only makes sense. You'll get used to payments and won't even notice them. I've found that if you think big, big things happen--the money just takes care of itself. If you think cheap, then you'll never get anywhere. Besides which, on this lease you don't have anything to worry about. The company's going to take care of all your routine maintenance for the full term. Now, would you like the 48 month or 60 month program?"

Feeling overwhelmed by Jim's high-pressure sales job, Bill remarks:

"You know . . . I'm just not ready to make this kind of commitment yet. I mean, this is really a big payment for me. This lease will actually cost me as much as my condo. I really have to go home and discuss it with my wife before making any decisions."

Showing impatience and sensing his customer's ambivalence, Jim tries even more pressure and says:

"OK Bill . . . this is an incredible deal I'm offering you. But it's only going to last today. Tomorrow is going to be a different deal. Today is the end of the month and I can offer you these savings. If you sign now, I'll throw in the carpeted car mats--but that's it. You'll never get another deal like this. What do you say?"

Still reeling from the first pitch and not yet cured of his misgivings, Bill says:

"Jim, I know you've made me a great deal, but I'm just not ready to sign. Let me go home and think on it--I'll call you tomorrow."

Now, we'll never know whether Bill ever called Jim back. But judging by his continued reluctance, all of Jim's added persuasion seems to have backfired. Hard-selling or pressuring works for some, but most individuals need to be cut more slack when making major purchases. Jim's insensitivity, presumptuousness, impatience and grandiosity seem to have hurt his cause. While Jim's 'a legend in his own mind,' the reality is that his numbers are considerably below expectations. His bravado hurts his chances of developing credibility and charisma because he's too defensive to absorb constructive feedback. Before he's even ready to counter objections, he needs to learn more empathy, sensitivity and attention to his client's needs.

In this particular case, Bill needed someone to give him permission to go through his own machinations over the 'big' purchase. Rather than blasting him with his neurosis, he should have slowed down a bit and shown more empathy. Instead of dominating the sales meeting, he should have listened attentively and validated that it's OK for Bill to have anxieties. Using the high-level intangibles of timing, tact, playfulness and humor, and certainly 'common sense,' he would have played his hand out differently. Instead of knowing it all, Jim might have experimented with a different approach. Trying a more patient but indirect strategy, he could say:

"Bill you seem like you're having some legitimate concerns about the purchase. Please feel free to ask me any questions you might have. I know that buying a car can be a huge decision. You seem like an intelligent, thoughtful individual. Only you are capable of knowing what's comfortable and best for you. I can only tell you from my other customers who've been in similar positions, it's not easy to make this kind of decision. But once they do, they seem to make the adjustment just fine. They're actually really happy with their purchase. But I just want you to know that if this doesn't feel right to you, then maybe it's best to hold off for now. There will always be other opportunities in the future."

Using a softer-sell approach seems to work with a larger percentage of possible buyers--whether it's selling intangibles like insurance or arranging contracts for professional athletes. Railroading people raises defensiveness and exacerbates ordinary opposition to unwanted levels, killing most deals. While it's easy to grow impatient, sales professionals should remind themselves that the dynamics of deal making involves a bilateral process taking into consideration the second party in the transaction. Tuning-in to the other person's needs--even if it means allowing them to equivocate--shows the kind of sensitivity and support needed to expand credibility and advance a deal toward a close. Losing sight of this agenda, imposing too much too soon and unduly pressuring prospects, usually backfires.

Once you've bonded with your customer, you'll be in a much better place to engage in standard closing techniques. Closing isn't an all or none proposition, namely, 'either take it or leave it.' Most closes involve a methodical--and sometimes arduous--process in which there's a series of small but significant steps toward the goal Each step along the way is systematically reinforced until the final goal is achieved. It's somewhat akin to animal training in which smaller, simpler units of behavior are shaped into more complex activities. Methodically using praise and validation, good negotiators know how to move people along toward the eventual close. Our car salesperson might direct his customer with the following sequence of responses:

1. "You seem like a person of great refinement and sophistication. Yes. That's very intelligent of you to have interest in this vehicle!" [reinforcement/validation]

2. "If I could help you get into any model, which one would it be? Yes. That's a very smart choice!" [reinforcement/validation]

3. "If we could keep your payments down to an affordable level, would you be interested in the car? Yes. You've really got good taste!" [reinforcement/validation]

4. "Wouldn't you agree, that the model you've selected is a great car? Yes. It's good that you're able to see that!" [reinforcement/validation]

5. "If you get your price and can afford the payments, doesn't buying/leasing the car make sense? Yes. That really shows great shopping savvy!"[reinforcement/validation]

6. "Now that we've gotten the payments you can afford, doesn't this seem more affordable than you thought? Yes. You've really made yourself a great deal!" [reinforcement/validation]

7. "After really examining all of these things, doesn't this deal make good sense? Yes. You've really put together a great deal!" [reinforcement/validation]

8. "Would you kindly review the contract and sign on the spots marked 'X?' Yes. You've made an outstanding purchase!" [reinforcement/validation]

Looking at the above hypothetical sequence, it's possible to see the chain of reinforcement leading to the eventual close. By methodically using incremental stages of positive reinforcement and validation, overwhelmingly large purchases can be broken down into manageable parts. Just like a good hiker looks no further than his next step, good deal makers, too, look at rewarding the many minor parts of the deal moving toward an eventual close. If you look too far ahead--regardless of the situation--you may never get there. How many couples look too far into the future, become frustrated, fail to achieve their goals and wind up breaking up? Plenty! If they'd spend more time focused on relating well in the present, the future would take care of itself. This is equally true with most other kinds of deal-making.

As we've seen, making deals and closing deals are two very different activities. Many people have the starting power, but they can't muster the staying or finishing power to achieve their goals. Taking goals in small increments helps to sustain the energy and motivation necessary to eventually succeed at the bigger picture. That only makes sense. When you bite off more than you can chew and try to do too much too soon, you're setting yourself up for failure. Pressing too much in sales situations tips your hand and reveals unwanted desperation, making closing a more difficult job. Showing empathy, consideration and patience and not pushing too hard creates a more inviting atmosphere in which to make deals.

Recognizing that there's a murky zone between self-confidence and narcissism, should remind most ambitious individuals that they must tiptoe around their propensity toward egotism. Grandiosity and arrogance kills most sales deals. While it's OK to be pumped with enthusiasm, it's still another to show so much hyperactivity that you risk offending others. Even as this is said, it needs to be pointed out that *everyone* is involved in some type of sales. Whether you're promoting a dental practice or video dating service, credibility and charisma are still at the heart of self-promotion. Regardless of the venue, incorporating *high-level intangibles* puts you on the right track.

'Right' Doesn't Always Make Like

Life isn't always a courtroom battle. When you walk away the victor, you're usually leaving behind the vanquished: A defeated person whose memory of humiliation doesn't die easily. Despite all your attempts at networking, you've turned loose an enemy whose major preoccupation is seeking your demise. It's difficult to develop credibility-- and its heir-apparent charisma--when you've generated so much antipathy that others are waiting for you to take a fall. Winning arguments is a losing battle in which your short-lived gains are another person's defeat. Although it's tempting to prove to the world your 'rightness,' it's also a risky strategy for building relationships.

Beating people at their own game is an art in which you have to let them save face. Reminding them of your superiority seems like it's healthy for the ego, but it's actually shortsighted and self-defeating. Good sportsmanship allows you to win but it doesn't permit you to pound your chest and humiliate others. While everyone wants to advance their agenda, narcissistic exhibitionism-- like pumping your fist at someone else's expense--should be avoided like radioactivity. Showing high-level intangibles like, tact, diplomacy, good judgment and sensitivity, automatically increase one's credibility and charisma.

Developing credibility is a tall order to fill if you're not well liked. And the surest path to not being liked is constantly proving that you're right at someone else's expense. While some people have an insatiable desire to be right, it's *politically incorrect* to argue and impose your will. Creating enemies and discouraging others comes back to haunt you. Watching others get mileage out of proving their 'correctness' shows a degree of immaturity incompatible with wielding lasting credibility and charisma. Let's face it, how 'smart' are you when you've alienated the very people who are potentially capable of helping you? Even when you think you're invincible and have no need for others' help, you still want people on your side. Having people pray for your downfall sets up some undesirable momentum, preempts successful networking and invites expectations of failure.

Creating your own luck is very much related to establishing amicable relationships in which people are opening doors--not slamming them in your face. Allowing your ego to pick useless fights sets a dangerous precedent. Remaining overly reactive and oblivious to what pushes your buttons doesn't promote the kind of methodical control needed to establish credibility and promote your agenda. How much credibility do you have when you're constantly over-reacting to the provocation of others? Charismatic people aren't back on their heels, they're always on the advance, plotting new strategies and conquering new goals.

Operating with a weakened and hyper-reactive ego places you on the defensive and renders you incapable of gleaning the bigger picture. Always putting out fires and managing crises, ego problems prevent individuals from establishing credibility and displaying charisma. If you're too busy defending yourself and constantly worrying about containing your enemies, you'll have a lot less energy to pursue your goals. Constantly distracted by persecutory anxieties, it's difficult to find a positive outlook. Instead, individuals with ego problems find the world an inhospitable place from which they're launching unprovoked attacks on innocent bystanders.

Viewing the world from a fragile ego, individuals feel attacked by even innocuous gestures, leaving them prone toward counterattacking others on inconsequential matters. How can you expect to be liked by others when you're always on the defensive? It's not very realistic. Proving that you're 'right' and defending yourself should take a back seat to finding special ways of meeting the needs of others. When you're too busy licking your own emotional wounds, it's unrealistic to be focused on helping others achieve their goals. And, clearly, if you're of no real use to others, they're not going to *like* you. Guess what? If you're not well liked--despite all your persuasive skills--you can forget about developing credibility and charisma.

People are viewed as credible when they're *liked*. You can possess all the credentials and information in the world, but, if you're not liked, your audience won't be listening. When others are indifferent, or, worse yet, hostile toward your interests, credibility won't be coming your way. How can you network and develop friendships when you have nothing good to say about people? Emotionally fragile individuals are known to criticize, condemn, denounce, attack and control people with whom they're involved. Breeding that kind of negativity surely usurps your credibility and charisma. Returning to a familiar case illustrates, this time around, problems with credibility.

A wealthy candidate for statewide office, whose personal fortune was made in the airline industry, boasted that his political campaign was almost entirely financed from his own savings. Claiming that he wasn't beholden to any special interests, he criticized his opponents for being in the pockets of various lobbying groups. Portraying his opponents as tax and spend liberals, he was the only candidate who had no personal ax to grind. Claiming that his desire to seek public service was purely altruistic, he stood to lose vast amounts of income by serving in public office. Often comparing himself to 20th century political icons, he claimed that his crusade for elected office was the restoration of political idealism. And yet, when pushed on clarifying his positions on important issues facing the voters, he deliberately equivocated, lest he alienate one group or another. During a televised debate he's asked some pointed questions by a contentious interviewer [Mr. Jones] who says:

"Mr. Davis, you've said that you wouldn't run a 'dirty' campaign, but your recent TV ads have portrayed your opponents as owned by corporations and major lobbying groups. You've even said that they're doing the bidding of multinational corporations. You've said yourself, that you're not obligated to anyone other than yourself. Your ads have also suggested that your opponents campaigns were financed with illegal campaign contributions. Can you tell the voters here tonight what proof you have of these allegations? Voters are also interested in your positions on affirmative action, education, illegal immigration, the medical use of marijuana, and the death penalty."

Feeling the heat, the voluble but defensive candidate [Mr. Davis] responds quickly saying:

"Mr. Jones, I'm the only candidate who spent nearly 100% of his own savings on his campaign. I just happen to believe that if you allow others to subsidize your campaign, they'll expect you to do their bidding. And because my opponents all received campaign contributions from the insurance lobby, NRA, medical associations, law enforcement groups, poultry farmers, public education unions, and the like, they're obligated to advance the agendas' of these groups. Now, as for my positions on these various issues, I've already stated my views to the voters."

Dissatisfied with the candidate's response and sensing that he was blowing smoke, the interviewer [Mr. Jones] takes another swipe and says:

"Mr. Davis, isn't it true that you're quick to condemn your opponents for accepting campaign contributions because you've solicited all those groups and came up blanks? Isn't it a fact that you've tried to solicit those groups, but not one of those groups or organizations contributed to your campaign because your positions are so out of step with the mainstream? Isn't that the real story?"

With his fuse getting short, the candidate [Mr. Davis] begins to lose his cool and barks back:

"No, No, No! That's absolutely not true! We decided early on in this campaign that it's better to subsidize your own cause so that you're not beholden to anyone. Because I've paid all the bills, the buck stops with me. My opponents want to duck the real issue of this campaign, and, that is, who's going to continue California's prosperity into the next millennium? Who better, than a multimillionaire businessman whose own personal fortune proves that he's capable of managing tax payers' money? My opponents are experts at *spending* money not making it."

Sensing the candidate's evasiveness on the real issues, the interviewer [Mr. Jones] tries again:

"Mr. Davis, while you claim that your opponents are obligated to vaious groups, you seem accountable to only one person--yourself. According to your view, we all know to whom your opponents are obligated. By the same logic, why should the electorate believe that you'll pursue anything other than your own agenda?"

Now even more over-reactive, the candidate [Mr. Davis] remarks:

"I know what's best for the electorate. If voters feel that the other candidates more accurately reflect their views, then I would suggest they consider voting for someone else."

Taking another tact, the interviewer [Mr. Jones] tries to get the candidate re-focused on responding to his original requests for clarification about his positions on important issues and asks:

"OK Mr. Davis, let's go back to your positions on gun control, affirmative action, medical use of marijuana, death penalty, bilingual education, illegal immigration, etc. Voters have a right to know your positions on these key issues."

Reluctant to hazard an opinion, the candidate [Mr. Davis] says:

"Mr. Jones, my positions on these issues are well known to anyone following my extensive TV ads. I don't think this is

the time and place to go into any further elaboration beyond
saying that I'm not going to get into divisive issues."

While the candidate presents with authoritative credentials,
his defensive responses don't improve his credibility. His
grandiosity, arrogance and superior attitude turn off viewers
sensing his reluctance to respond on key issues. Rather than
state his positions, he adopts the view that taking a position
is divisive and promotes bad publicity. His imperious
ridicule of his opponents on the issue of campaign financing
has backfired, since it's now exposed that, in point of fact,
he couldn't raise any campaign contributions on his own.
Condemning other candidates for their obligations to
lobbyists is now replaced by anxieties that this candidate
isn't accountable to anyone.

Establishing credibility is a sensitive balance between
sharing authoritative information and making a favorable
presentation. When you're deprecating others, it doesn't
reflect favorably on yourself. Certainly displaying
narcissistic propensities transforms an otherwise appealing
person into one quite offensive and unlikable. Since
credibility and charisma are closely correlated with being
well liked, conspicuous selfishness assures that you'll be
seen as unattractive and unappealing. Developing a likable
personality involves rewarding people and making them feel
special. Most people like hearing positive things about
themselves. This should come as no surprise. Although
some have errantly concluded that 'flattery will get you
nowhere,' most people know that this doesn't match reality.

More realistically, if flattery is perceived as insincere or
viewed as a means of manipulation, then it's not going to be
very effective. But, even that involves a big assumption that
the perception of manipulation isn't out-weighed by the ego
gratification derived from receiving flattery. Paying

compliments--whether they're true or not--is a powerful form of validation rarely exceeded even by the riches obtained from money. Most people will work harder, expend more energy, and stay committed to causes due to special recognition and approval than for only monetary rewards. Puzzling as this sounds, the workplace--regardless of the field--is replete with judgment and criticism and has a veritable shortfall of approval and validation. Most people seldomly get their needs for approval and validation met on the job.

Finding a source of approval and validation is like locating your very own gold mine for your self-esteem. Whether it's found in love relationships, friendships, work relationships or any other place, people usually hang on to it at all costs. If you're looking for lasting relationships, offer abundant approval and compliments and you'll find an army of loyal followers who won't let you go. Just as surely, if you want a high turnover in business or social relationships, infect people with a profusion of disapproval and criticism. Arguing, challenging, confronting, competing, criticizing, ridiculing and nit-picking assure that you'll wind up a very lonely person. Rather than proving that 'you're right,' prove that you're capable of elevating a person's self-worth by showing unconditional approval and validation.

Many managers--or even parents--are wondering how can you possibly reward behavior which doesn't conform to your own standards or expectations of perfection? Short of fulfilling this benchmark, giving praise seems phony and undeserved. You can rest assured that by giving healthy doses of approval and validation, you'll get a lot more mileage out of your subordinates or superiors. Think of offering approval and validation as your main reinforcement by which you sculpt others in the mold of your own expectations. If you want instant credibility and charisma, don't wait until you get exactly what you want. Begin immediately applying powerful social reinforcements to shape your own destiny.

A charismatic criminal defense attorney, known for his evangelical oratory, whose impeccable appearance and folksy communication style played well with judges and juries, defends a well known celebrity accused of a double homicide. With the prosecution mounting a formidable case, presenting what appears as incontrovertible evidence, he continues his relentless pursuit of winning the hearts and minds of the jury. Displaying lavish praise and abundant compliments, he says:

"Ladies and gentlemen, with your permission . . . you'all weren't born yesterday. You're intelligent people. No one-- not the prosecution, the police or the experts--has a better understanding of this case than you do. You've heard all the fancy experts; listened to all the detectives; inspected all the evidence; even tried to make some logical sense of the police, detectives and criminalists; and, now, only *you* are capable of applying all the common sense needed to reach your verdict. No one should discount your smarts. You'all know there's something wrong . . . something terribly wrong with the police's story. They're asking you to believe that Mr. Jones was stupid enough to leave a blood trail from the murder scene to his home and, then, to take the most incriminating piece of evidence and drop it on his property. . . and yet the murder weapon, shoes and bloody clothing were never found. The police are also asking you to believe in disappearing and reappearing blood drops and DNA testing which contains the same chemical present in the police's treated blood samples. Really! You're different than the police or the prosecution. You'all are committed to finding the truth. No one's capable of misleading you, no matter how convincing they seem. Only you are capable of

seeing through all the lies and cover-ups . . . I know you'll
do the right thing. Let's send the police a lasting message. I
have faith in each and every one of you."

Charming the jury with abundant approval and validation,
the savvy defense attorney knows that his credibility and
charisma are weighted on being liked. His statements were
highly respectful and heavily complimentary, attesting often
to the jury's intelligence and wisdom. He's cognizant of the
fact that if he's well liked--with all else being equal--he'll
eventually receive the benefit of the doubt. He knows that
avoiding rancor, pettiness and unprovoked attacks--and
showing abundant humor--his complimentary demeanor
eventually pays off. Like most politicians, he knows that
the more upbeat he appears, the more negative his
opponents seem by contrast. Maintaining his sense of
humor, remaining positive, and displaying high levels of
approval and validation, helps orchestrate his agenda.

Compared to the defense, the prosecution's methodical
presentation appeared too robotic and insensitive. Unlike
the defense, prosecutors' presentations were less 'human'
and tinged with disbelief, criticism and even ridicule. The
defense's down-to-earth, folksy presentation was contrasted
sharply with prosecutors' authoritative, scientific and more
sterile approach. Missing were the endearing *faux pas* and
solicitations of sympathy. Responding in closing arguments
prosecutors summarize their case:

"Ladies and gentlemen . . . the defense has failed to deliver
any of their promises made in opening arguments. All their
witnesses either disappeared or were entirely discredited;
all their theories were thoroughly disproven; and the
evidence proved that the defendant was guilty beyond any
reasonable doubt. You've seen all their theories turned
upside down: Colombian drug hit men, rogue cops, police

frame-ups, random gang killings, etc. The defense's contentions were never proven, and, by any rational person's standards, are preposterous. You've seen the indisputable evidence and listened to the experts. They've all told you the same thing: No one other than the defendant is responsible for these killings. The defense has blown a lot of smoke, but none of you can ignore the truth. The blood and DNA don't lie. You've seen it with your own eyes. You can't deny what's in your face. Although you may like the defendant and know him to be a different person, you can't ignore what you've seen. You, the jury, must look at the facts and only the facts. What you feel is not relevant to rendering your verdict. We've presented you the best evidence, now you must put all emotions aside and make your judgment. The people of the state of California are counting on you . . ."

Although many of these statements might be factually correct, they're *politically incorrect* to the extent that they don't display adequate tact, diplomacy and appropriate sensitivity. From the jury's perspective, they've heard both sides. Why should they automatically favor one set of evidence over the other? Disparaging the defense's case paradoxically raises doubts in the jury's mind about the prosecution's credibility. Why the need to denigrate so forcefully the other side if they really have a strong case? Shouldn't the facts speak for themselves? While attempting to bolster their own credibility, the prosecution inadvertently administered self-inflicted wounds. Rather than appearing as likable and appealing, their overly dour presentation turns off jurors who otherwise might have been receptive. In the end, what really mattered: The 'facts' or the way in which they're presented? You know the answer!

Ignoring *high-level intangibles*--like tact, timing, diplomacy, empathy, consideration and 'common sense'--

risks paying the heavy price of alienating people. Impressing people with all the facts is no guarantee of success--especially if you've turned off your audience. Relating and asserting credibility are closely connected with executing the many high-level intangible responsible for effective communication. Without paying attention to these special qualities, you may be 'right' but you won't be liked. And, as we've said, if you're not liked, orchestrating your agenda is going to be like rowing without oars..

Paying a little more attention to giving approval and validation might be the difference--regardless of the situation--between success and failure. While it's more 'natural' to level criticisms, it's far more productive to give recognition and support. Even when it goes against your grain, just remind yourself of your goals. Think to yourself: How am I going to enlist friends, orchestrate people and achieve my goals? Can I do it on my own? Or, do I need the help of people at my disposal? Why suffer the indignity of isolation and low popularity? Focus your attention away from yourself and onto making others' lives more rewarding--no matter how insignificantly. Being liked can be as simple as springing for a few unsolicited compliments. It's certainly worth the price.

Some Final Thoughts

Credibility, like personality, is a labile essence which is easily vaporized. Both credibility and charisma go together like a tie with a suit. Resembling fine wine, credibility takes time to mature and develop character and is easily soured by the wrong conditions. One wrong move, one brief lapse of consciousness, one mistake, one blunder, one simple miscalculation, can transform a lifetime of hard work and good reputation into a tragic calamity. What's also ironic is the fact that sometimes having too much history hurts credibility because one's reputation, no matter how bullet-proof, isn't entirely missing its chinks. Over the course of anyone's career, catching some adverse publicity--like the common cold--is a *fait accompli*.

Impeccable credentials are no guarantee that credibility will either be established or maintained. At best, impressive credentials help create a baseline of credibility only to be tested by an individual's actual presentation. With credibility, 'you can run but you can't hide.' Eventually you must come out and face your audience, and they're forced to form their own impression. There are no surrogates when it comes to credibility. While credibility can be temporarily transferred to you designated representatives, e.g., agents, attorneys, publicists, press secretaries, etc., eventually the buck stops with the acts of the person whose credibility is on the line.

For some people wiping the slate clean and starting over fresh offers the hope of renewed credibility. For others, it's just a fantasy. Occasionally, memories are short and sometimes forgiving. For the vast majority, credibility isn't entirely destroyed when mistakes occur. Like the ocean temperature, there's a constancy or stability factor at play. It takes considerable disruption to entirely torpedo one's credibility. But short of a total personality change, when credibility is vitiated, even the best damage control strategies yield unsatisfactory results. Obviously, the best strategy for maintaining credibility is preempting costly mistakes.

Credibility differs from reputation in that the latter represents more a historical track-record establishing a long-term pattern of behavior. Credibility requires no such track-record. Individuals can have extraordinary credibility without a distinguished or notorious reputation. While reputation is certainly correlated with credibility, you can still have a favorable reputation with mediocre credibility. More akin to image, credibility conjures impressions of power, wealth, brilliance and trust. It's possible to look the part and say and do all the right things and establish strong credibility. In fact, credibility often decays quickly when you actually get to know someone over time.

Credibility is a game of consistency. As long as someone appears consistent and doesn't deviate too far from expectations, then credibility is usually preserved. Damaging credibility occurs easily when contradictory information emerges, leading to the impression that the person isn't telling the truth or no longer performs consistent with their reputations. With enough contradictory information, credibility quickly turns South. Maintaining consistency is also essential for preserving one's image--an essential feature to exhibiting charisma.

Maintaining a positive image involves more than flying by the seat of your pants and hoping for the best: It requires methodical planning and calculation. Nothing upends credibility more than unresolved unconscious conflicts. When you're not conscious of your emotions and certain beliefs, unwanted behavior occurs when you least expect it. It might be inappropriate emotional outbursts, impulsive sexual behavior, shoplifting, blurting out ill-advised statements, clouded judgment or a host of other counterproductive acts, which wind up sabotaging credibility. Better control of unconscious dynamics enables otherwise self-defeating individuals to remain on track. Failure to gain better control of the submerged part of the 'iceberg' damages credibility and weakens charisma.

Apart from gaining better control over unconscious dynamics, advancing credibility involves learning appropriate ways of self-promoting. Incorporating *high-level intangibles*, e.g., tact, timing, good judgment, 'common sense,' energy and enthusiasm, politeness and good manners, etc., improves the talent of promoting credibility and developing charisma. Without using high-level intangibles, the path toward developing credibility and charisma is poorly marked. Showing healthy altruism and remaining focused on expanding the success of others is the best formula for gaining charisma.

Ultimately developing credibility is related to being liked. All the technical skill and knowledge at your disposal can't compensate for an unlikable personality. One of the most certain ways to torpedo credibility and charisma is remaining too focused on your own selfish agenda. While your goals might be to advance your own cause, it's going to be a rough ride if you're perceived as too self-serving. It's no accident that if you do the little things that help others, your popularity will soar together with your attractiveness. At the end of the day, you can't talk about developing credibility and charisma if you're not well liked.

Points to Remember

- Remain focused on expanding the success of others

- Avoid grandiose, arrogant and selfish displays

- Make plausible explanations whenever possible

- Develop awareness and sensitivity of your impact on others

- Reduce the gap between how you're seen by yourself and others

- Identify and deal with unresolved unconscious conflicts and emotions

- Open yourself to receiving constructive feedback

- Recognize and complete 'unfinished business'

- Work toward making the unconscious conscious

- Present your best side without appearing narcissistic

- Use validation and praise while interacting with others

- Refrain from engaging in excessive self-deprecation

- Display self-confidence without showing conceit or superiority

- Find ways of making people feel special

- Avoid criticism and ridicule whenever possible

- Show recognition, offer approval and give validation abundantly

- Use high-level intangibles while attempting to orchestrate your agenda

Chapter 5

CHARISMA INSIDE-OUT

In this chapter you'll learn about the other side of charisma and how it differs from manipulation • Introduction • The other side of charisma • Charisma and manipulation • Putting it all together • Some final thoughts • Points to remember • Some concluding thoughts

Introduction

Before examining the other side of charisma--the dynamics of individuals drawn toward its magnetic properties--it's necessary to comment about some prevailing fallacies. The first involves the notion that charisma doesn't really exist. While scientific verification isn't yet possible, most people know intuitively when they're exposed to charisma. Like the force of gravity, its presence is unmistakable and no less powerful. When encountering it, you feel the energy, excitement, awe and inspiration. It's just there and you know it. Convinced by personal experience that charisma exists, others question whether it's possible to *learn* its many essential features. On that note, OPERATION CHARISMA makes its strongest case: Yes, the elements of charisma can be taught.

After considerable discussion, it should be clear that charisma is a mercurial but essential property which waxes and wanes depending on the situation. Although many people would like to believe that charisma is genetically endowed and remains constant throughout a lifetime, we've seen too many examples of how it's neglected, abused and

eventually lost.   Or, as circumstances change, the person
falls off the pedestal along with all the charisma. While it's
true that genetic programming plays a part, we've also seen
that everyday events change the picture.   There's no
question that charisma, like math skills, comes more
naturally to some people than others. In the final analysis, it
doesn't really matter whether charisma is inborn or learned:
What counts is whether you're able to use it to advance your
agenda.

Having innate talent means that charisma is learned more
easily, but it doesn't suggest, by any stretch, that it can't be
learned. Nor does it indicate that native ability--whether it's
intelligence, beauty, personality or anything else--will thrive
in a vacuum. Like anything else, charisma needs to be
nurtured. Without proper cultivation, it dies like a flower in
parched earth. Countless examples of what seems like
dramatic personality transformations occur on a regular
basis escaping our attention.   How many 'nerdy' people
from your childhood are now beautiful models or actors,
powerful corporate executives, dynamic physicians, talented
musicians, artists or writers, successful business people, or
other success stories which defied initial predictions? More
than you're willing to admit! Attending enough high school
reunions proves this out. Shaking your head, you just can't
believe that the 'best and the brightest' often look the most
'aged and tired' and the ones at whom you wouldn't give a
second look are now in the limelight.

A likable, conforming, overweight, non-athletic young
man, whose popularity was nothing to write home about and
whose accomplishments were equally uneventful, exited
high school with little fanfare. Not voted 'most likely to
succeed,' he floundered in college, drifting aimlessly from
one major to another. During his junior year, a friend of his
father's offered him an unglamorous menial job at a well

known Hollywood movie studio. Starting at the bottom but, soon finding himself a mentor, he became a loyal lieutenant to one of the studios' upcoming movie executives. Riding along with his boss's meteoric rise to nearly the top, he eventually wound up the chief of the company's most prestigious film subsidiaries. After getting considerable press, he received endless streams of unreturnable phone calls from alleged 'friends' he didn't even know. Deciding to attend his 20 year high school reunion, his presence was looked upon with great anticipation. Attending the reunion, he's surrounded by an obsequious group of admiring classmates delighting in re-establishing old acquaintances which never really existed. At the evening reception, he's found talking to one of his class's most popular cheerleaders who says:

" Joey, I can't believe it's been 20 years since graduation. You look fabulous! I've heard you've been keeping yourself busy lately. Your life seems really exciting. I've even seen your name on the credits of a number of movies. You probably heard, I married Johnny [her high school sweetheart] but we've been divorced for several years. Things just didn't work out."

Looking distracted and a little bored with the conversation, Joey says:

"You're right Adrian, I haven't heard a thing about you. It's too bad that you guys split up. I remember--way back when--wanting to go out with you. I guess that's what everybody wanted at the time. Things just never worked out. You're right I have been busy. I really love what I'm doing. It's great working on projects which seem to have so much impact on people. I really couldn't imagine myself doing anything else. It's really interesting getting to know many of the actors and artists working on the pictures. How about you? Are you happy?"

Buzzing with excitement and mesmerized with his attention, Adrian remarks:

"I'm working as a legal secretary. And, no, I'm *not* really happy. I never imagined my life would wind up like this. It's great that you love what you do! I guess I'm still trying to find myself. Maybe I can get involved in something you're doing? Would you mind if I gave you a call sometime after the reunion? Maybe we could get together for a drink or something?"

Reacting with muted enthusiasm, Joey says:

"Adrian, that would be great! I'd love to get together. I'll be out of town during the remainder of June, but give me a call sometime in July and we'll try to set something up."

Shortly after the reunion, Adrian reads that there's been a major shake-up at the studio. One of the main casualties was Joey's boss. He apparently had a falling out with the studio chief and abruptly tendered his 'resignation.' Inside sources say he was summarily dismissed. Along with his boss, Joey was also headed for the unemployment lines. Having taken a 180 degree change of plans, Joey decides to call Adrian.

He calls and leaves her a message. Sometime later, she returns his call and says:

"Joey, I read about what happened--I'm really sorry. What are you going to do?"

Still in a mild state of shock the otherwise considerate Joey is consumed with anxiety and remarks:

"You know Adrian . . . I really don't know. There's a lot of possibilities. Right now, I've contacted my attorney and it's all in his hands. There's really nothing I can do at this point. I'm really sorry that I'm no longer in any position to be discussing how *you* can fit in. I'm not even sure at this point where I'll end up. I don't have a clue what my boss is going to do. I think this whole thing had to do with politics. His boss was scared that he [my boss] was going after his job . . . well you know the ways these things work. Everyone's paranoid. Anyway, enough of this stuff . . . I guess I've got some extra time now. When is it good to get together for that 'drink?'"

After absorbing a mega-dose of Joey's anxieties and distress, Adrian's enthusiasm seems to dampen and she says:

"You know Joey, this week is really bad for me. My boss has loaded me down with so many projects. I'll be a wreck by the end of the week. Let me call you next week after the dust finally settles."

As we can see, charisma vacillates like the stock market depending on the situation. When on the top, Joey appears attractive, stimulating and highly desirable. He's dripping with personal power. After abruptly losing his position, his charisma seems to evaporate, despite the fact that he's the very same person. Sharing his frustrations with Adrian clearly turns her off to the point that 'going out for a drink' no longer has much appeal. While she would have accommodated *his* busy schedule before, it's now her busy schedule which prompts the postponement of the meeting. Although his personality has some appeal, without the 'magic' of his position, his high energy, enthusiasm and attractiveness tarnishes quickly. Despite being a 'nice guy,' with all his current problems, he no longer has the same pizzazz. When you're on the top, it's a whole different story. What's important to note is the fact that charisma is clearly affected by circumstances.

Having popularity and charisma at one stage of your life is no guarantee that it will continue. Many people accept 'scripts' written and performed at early stages of their lives by people they don't even know or by major influences--like parents, siblings, relatives or teachers--whose power and influence have absolutely no relevance in their lives today. OPERATION CHARISMA assumes that anyone with normal intelligence and enough motivation is capable of applying the *high-level intangibles* to transform their lives. By paying more attention to improving these unlabeled talents, developing charisma is both realistic and eminently doable.

The specific and verifiable ways in which a person acts, namely, the way they apply *high-level intangibles*, directly impacts the presence and level of charisma. In other words, without consistently applying high-level intangibles, charisma fades like an old photograph: It becomes a tired and worn image. To retain its vibrancy and color, it must be carefully nurtured by executing the right high-level intangibles. If it were really true that charisma was purely inborn, then it wouldn't be possible to cultivate it--and we know that this isn't in the case.

Too many people have proved that by working on improving high-level intangibles, charisma and all its many rewards begin to materialize, despite all the self-doubt and apprehensions. Absorbing only 10% of these high-level intangibles, can make a dramatic difference in one's charisma and attainment of important goals. Controlling negative thinking isn't wholly necessary, since adherence to the program--i.e., incorporating high-level intangibles--takes care of many of the suspicions and doubts. The results become self-evident.

While it's helpful to retain the greatest percentage of information possible, only small amounts--about 10%--can mean the difference between success or failure. No one's evaluating you: Why should you be grading yourself? Of course, everyone wants some measure of their progress, and there's nothing wrong with that. But mercilessly berating yourself for not being perfect isn't helpful. Employ high-level intangibles in whatever ways possible and your life will never be the same. Learning new things really does make a difference!

The Other Side of Charisma

So far we've explored the many *high-level intangibles* and essential aspects of charisma. What we haven't focused on closely is the relationship between charismatic people and their many loyal followers. Without their adoring fans, charismatic people lose their magic, because if they've got no one to influence, and their special powers can't be fully appreciated. Like a teacher without a classroom, charismatic people lose their personal power when they're missing an audience. Like all artists, athletes, politicians and others, charismatic people thrive on audience involvement.

While it's possible for artists, musicians, writers, athletes or politicians to execute their crafts without an audience, it's like a romance without a partner: Hugging yourself can only go so far. How can you achieve your potential as a politician, for instance, without a following? It can't be done. And charisma or other forms of artistic expression can't be completely developed or satisfied without a devoted following. Keeping an audience interested involves careful recognition of their specific needs. Clearly if an artist, politician, or whatever has no regard for his audience, then the 'devoted' following loses interest in their work. The artist's work--like that of a good doctor--accurately diagnoses and treats the specific needs of the customers.

When the audience pays attention and shows appreciation, it has performance-enhancing effects. No one can fulfill their creative or charismatic potential without some measure of outside recognition and approval. Believing that artists or athletes function without recognition is like believing that fish swim without water. Although artistic works certainly have a life of their own, they can't reach full expression without a body of outside admirers. Throughout the book, that's why so much emphasis has been placed on abandoning narcissism, adopting altruism and addressing the unique needs of your audience--even if it's only an audience of one. As long as you're centered on meeting your own needs, it's going to be difficult to sustain charisma, since charisma involves directing your energy toward someone other than yourself.

Audiences have different kinds of needs and special expectations. Individuals drawn toward charismatic leaders vary in their needs but are almost always seeking out an answer to their problems. Whether the problems are financial, medical, emotional or spiritual, individuals are attracted toward those promising to cure their special unsatisfied needs. Whatever the special needs, you'll find some charismatic person catering to those deficits. It's no accident that some people, saddled with debt and strapped with unending money problems, are drawn toward financial gurus whose promises of riches and 'the good life' seem irresistible.

For people seeking out charisma, they tend to transfer all their unmet neediness onto a charismatic leader and energize them with magical powers. Looking to be rescued conjures powerful images, whether one's expectations are real or purely fantasy. Many disenfranchised individuals, whose families offer little support and whose histories of painful rejection and neglect leave them craving help, are especially vulnerable to charismatic leadership. Their emotional neediness is transferred to individuals and groups promising to satisfy their unmet needs.

In these scenarios, individuals are automatically saturated with charisma, without too much regard to how well charismatic leaders execute high-level intangibles. In other words, needy people tend to project all their rescue fantasies onto the available objects--whether groups or individuals. If leaders show unconditional love, support, empathy, consideration and undivided attention, the vulnerable person becomes easily infatuated and even mesmerized. But even with completely inept attempts at charismatic leadership, desperate followers create their own faulty beliefs: They see and hear what they believe, and they *believe* what they see and hear.

It's with these cases, in which abysmal neediness dictates a person's emotional responses, that some argue that charisma--as an independent phenomenon--is an illusion. Created out of anxiety and helplessness, some people manufacture exaggerated perceptions of personal power. They become euphoric and intoxicated by individuals promising to relieve them of their misery. In case you're wondering, this doesn't sound all that much different from fantasies created in romantic love relationships. Mired in the throws of infatuation [from the Greek word meaning *foolish*], many people know that love is blind. Regardless of how much anyone questions your judgment or begs you to see reality, you continue seeing with your heart. Only after your feelings sour, do you begin to see what everyone was talking about. As your emotions recede, you're finally able to pull back your projections and see reality.

A disgruntled accountant, Sam, frustrated with his career and having gone through a painful divorce, finds himself with a loss of meaning in his life. Losing his family and no longer living with his children, he develops depression leaving him lethargic and hopeless. After his divorce, he finds many of his long-time 'friends' no longer interested in getting together. Even his own parents, with whom he had a tenuous relationship while he was married, weren't interested in hearing his problems. Blaming him for his marital failure, they were even less tolerant and more rejecting following his divorce. As his depression worsened and he was rapidly losing his interest in life, he went to his M.D. for help. His doctor put him on Prozac, hoping that it would change his dysphoric mood. Jolting him out of his lethargy, the medication helped him get back on his computer. While surfing 'the net,' he found a website about UFO's promising love, utopia and salvation. The website read:

"INTERESTED IN A NEW LIFE? UFO's ARE REAL! MAKE YOUR RESERVATION NOW TO BEGIN YOUR LIFE OVER AGAIN"

Intrigued by the ad, Sam contacted the website which gave further information inviting interested parties to a celestial 'party' commemorating the arrival of Hale-Bopp comet. He attended the 'party' where he was greeted by two solicitous young women, both of whom warmly invited him to attend an exciting lecture about the dawning of the new age. Escorted into a small, semicircular lecture hall, he observed a movie screen with a projected image of a flying saucer riding on what appeared to be the tail of a streaking celestial body. Playing in the background was Debussy's *Snowflakes Are Dancing*, an enchanting magic carpet ride of dancing notes, harking him back to a past-life regression therapy session in which he tried to understand his karma and re-connect with some of his early-life pain. For an instant he remembered his mother's smiling face, an image disrupted in childhood due to her untimely death of cancer when he was 5. He was suddenly wrenched out of his reverie by the hypnotic voice of the keynote speaker:

"Today, you have the chance to join an historic event. Our group has made reservations to begin its celestial journey traveling in a UFO on the tail of the Hale-Bopp comet. We've already begun preparations for this momentous event. Those of you with courage will join us in our rendezvous with destiny. The rest of you should leave now and follow a different path. We're privileged to accept our meeting with eternity. We'll be traveling at the speed of light and will be transformed into pure energy becoming at one with the universe. It's time, my fellow travelers, to begin preparations for our journey . . ."

The leader's 'visionary' eyes and resonant voice appear slightly impatient as if he were late for a flight. Pulling himself out of his semi-torpid state, Sam begins to experience traces of the old depression and anxieties from which he's trying to escape. While he's intrigued by the charismatic leader's offer, his propensity toward procrastination leaves him wanting to take a second look. Feeling guilty and 'gutless,' he leaves the auditorium filled with remorse that he didn't have the nerve to follow his path into destiny. Within 48 hours, he reads the headline in the local newspaper:

"29 MEMBERS OF NEW AGE CULT DIE IN APPARENT MASS SUICIDE"

While Sam is still saying his hail Marys, he's shocked to find out that he attended a meeting of a secular cult whose charismatic leader persuaded his following to take a lethal cocktail of yogurt, honey and *cyanide*. He told them that only freeing the body by death could emancipate their spirits to join the UFO following the tail of the Hale-Bopp comet. Shocking as it seems, his loyal and faithful following believed his madness. Was his charisma so powerful that his worshipper's believed his every word, or, more shocking, did they believe their own delusions spawned from their abysmal neediness? On closer inspection, many disenfranchised souls, abandoned by their family and friends and walking wounded through life, are susceptible to the tempting promises made by cults and other fanatical groups.

Charismatic leaders can certainly sell farfetched and dangerous ideas and accelerate recruitment into these fanatical groups, but it's the vulnerable person's clouded judgment that usually gets one into trouble. As with Sam, when someone's down-and-out, starving for affection, support and, yes, food, and unable to meet the exigencies of survival, they're often in a weakened state. Looking to relieve their distress, they sometimes become involved with misleading and dangerous individuals or groups promising salvation or a utopian way of life. Teenagers, exposed to chaotic family backgrounds, lacking structure and support and desperately pursuing their identities, are especially vulnerable to radical groups offering empty promises. So too are stressed-out or mentally ill individuals having difficulty surviving, either already homeless or heading in that direction.

Under these circumstances, it's difficult to tell what exact role charisma plays in recruiting desperate individuals into cults and other fanatical groups. More likely, poor judgment and bad reality-testing, stemming from a failed adjustment to stressful circumstances, are equally responsible for why people are pulled into the orbit of dangerous groups. 'If there's a need, then there's a master,' is the prevailing notion in the relationship between charisma and vulnerable individuals. Whatever the need, some sociopath always has the answer. Knowing this, it's probably impossible to completely extricate the seller [the one with influence] from the buyer [the one with need] or, put another way, the leader from the follower. Both play an integral part in the phenomena of persuasion and influence.

When someone tries to sell you a bill of goods, who's ultimately responsible for making 'the sale?' Is it the buyer or seller? Sellers' tend to apply various methods of persuasion when attempting to close a deal. They may exaggerate the benefits of goods or services, namely, only focus on the positive attributes of the sale. Focusing on only the positive aspects of the sale reduces the beginning stages of buyer's remorse. Following commitment to the sale-- whether it's joining a gym or a cult--salespeople try to continue the buyer's focus on the positive aspects of the purchase. In so doing, clever salespeople convince buyers that they've made a wise decision. Clearly, this calculated strategy of reducing buyer's remorse is a form of manipulation.

Simultaneously, without any influence from the seller, the buyer's own mind plays some interesting tricks. Like the seller, the buyer's own personality, too, tries to persuade the individual that one made the right choice. This defense mechanism--also known as rationalization or *cognitive dissonance*--helps preserve the person's self-worth by convincing him, in effect, 'you're smart and you've made a great decision,' irrespective of whether that's actually true. So also working against dealing with reality, is a part of the personality which--like the charismatic leader--hoodwinks or tricks the person into believing that one acted intelligently.

In Sam's case, he fortunately decided to pass on the charismatic leader's offer of 'shedding his physical shell.' His observing ego or rational mind might have saved his life.   Life or death situations don't constitute the vast majority of situations involving persuasion and influence. Maintaining healthy skepticism and questioning various uncertain proposals, help inject more caution about accepting lock, stock and barrel either suspicious people or tempting offers.   Usually--but not always--the harder the sell, the more suspicious the proposition. Many people have heard 'that if something looks too good to be true, then it probably isn't,' underscoring the fact that before you conclude that you've got such wonderful luck, you'd better consider the reality of the situation.

A hard working but struggling, attractive, 35 year old, manicurist spent the better part of her working life [over 15 years] squirreling away money attempting to save a down payment to buy a home. Frequently working nights and weekends, she scrimped and saved over $50,000.00, a formidable sum considering it was mostly from tips. Having little success finding Mr. Right, she nonetheless prayed for the day she would meet someone matching her standards. She worked hard for the modicum of success she enjoyed and vowed she'd never compromise and become involved with someone less ambitious than she. Exposed to many different men through a popular video dating service, she was yet to find someone who met her standards. Impressed with good dressers and smooth talkers, she finally met a man she couldn't resist. He exceeded all her fantasies: He was handsome, charming, well educated, ostensibly hard working, garrulous, well mannered, impeccably dressed and, most of all, the glibbest talker she'd ever met. A stock broker by trade, he claimed to have dabbled in various investments. Oozing with 'charisma,' she fell madly in love with the man who came from nowhere to rescue her from her misery. After a few dates, he had already moved into her apartment and they were soon discussing marriage. Strapped for cash, but feigning a certain level of affluence, he urged her to take her $50,000.00 life-savings and invest it on a 'hot' insider stock tip on a high-tech auto-security company. She resisted at first, but reluctantly acquiesced to his persuasive belief that she stood to quadruple her investment within a couple of months of trading. Believing his smoke, she coughed up the cash. Trying to reassure her he says:

"Marge, you're making the most important decision of your life. You've decided to no longer be a slave to your own earnings--you're going to finally be financially secure. No longer are you going to worry about meeting your monthly expenses. With this investment, you'll be able to retire when *you* want. This is a very smart move. This investment will be like an annuity for your future. Unlike so many others, you've got the nerve to make this happen. You're truly someone who can see ahead!"

Still showing a tinge of apprehension, Marge says:

"Marv, I know there are no guarantees . . . but this is my life-savings. I've sweated-out and saved this money over the last 15 years. I just hope that I'm doing the right thing. I guess, nothing ventured is nothing gained. I know you've got to take risks to get ahead."

Sensing Marge's lingering doubts and possible equivocation, Marv takes a different tact and moves in on the close and remarks:

"Marge, I've always told you--investing isn't for everybody. You have to have the stomach for taking calculated risks. Very few people ever achieve a secure future. Maybe you're not one of those people. This investment may not be right for you. If you have any reservations, I would suggest you pass on this opportunity. I'm really not comfortable taking your money unless you're 100% convinced it's the right thing. Let's postpone this deal. Maybe at some point in the future another deal might come up. OK?"

Triggering a host of reactions and feeling that this was, more than ever, the right move, Marge says:

"Marv, I'm *not* getting cold feet! I'm more convinced than ever that this is the right thing to do. You've got my blessings--here's my check."

A short time after making the investment, Marge learned that the bottom fell out of the stock's value. The price took a nose dive from $50.00 per share down to an abysmal $10.00 per share. Her original $50,000 investment was now worth a piddling $10,000. Together with her stock plummeting, her hopes and dreams of a more secure future also crashed and burned. Feeling devastated by the 'unexpected' turn of events, she calls her broker to try to get all the facts. She phones him in a panic and says:

"Marv, what in God's name happened? How is it possible for this stock to drop this quickly? You were talking about its value shooting through the $100.00 per share ceiling. And now this? I can't believe what's happened. Isn't there anything you can do? I'm absolutely floored!"

Showing no signs of being rattled, Marv responds in a collected way:

"Marge--I'm really sorry for what happened. As I told you before, you've got to have the stomach for this kind of investing. As easily as the stock dropped, it might have just as easily taken off. You haven't really lost anything--it's just on paper. You weren't planning on cashing in your investment until retirement. Guess what? Over time, your investment is bound to come back and move ahead. You really have to take the long-range picture. Stop watching the stock tables, it'll drive you crazy! The market's ups and downs don't mean anything. Over the next several years, you'll see--you'll come out ahead. That's always the market's long-term trend--upward."

Marv's charm and persuasive skills were ratcheted up to new levels. Rather than talking her into the risky 'hot' stock investment, he began by talking her out of the investment. When he set enough 'reverse psychology' in motion to quell her ambivalence, he then validated her for her wisdom and intelligence. With the 'reverse psychology,' he created the impression that he could take or leave her investment and suddenly all her misgivings vanished. She was motivated to take the plunge. While these added persuasion techniques don't always go with charisma, they act like accelerants helping crafty manipulators advance their agendas.

After Marge's stock dropped like a rock, Marv's responses seem transparently specious as he tries to convince her that her losses will eventually turn into long-term gains. Using all his 'charisma,' he reminds her of the risks and reassures her that she only took a paper loss. While his arguments sound lucid, they're methodical attempts to reduce his exposure by minimizing the role he played in conning her into taking the risk. As Marge begins to re-examine where she went wrong, she'll see that her own neediness and fantasies of future wealth, robbed her of the analytical ability to fully appreciate what she was doing. While no one should discount Marv's role, they shouldn't minimize Marge's responsibility in attributing 'magical' powers to her 'well-intentioned' investment advisor. Clearly, Marv used his charisma and persuasive skills to push Marge into her decision, but Marge was also at-risk because of her own neediness.

As we can see, there's an interplay between the charismatic person and the individual to whom they're applying their manipulative skills. While discussing the 'iceberg' or role of unconscious processes in leaving individuals vulnerable to influence, it's easy to see how they're manipulated. Even with deficient charismatic skills, Marv still prevailed because Marge's reasoning was distorted by her overwhelming desires for security and wealth. It's difficult--as with romantic love relationships--to enlighten individuals when they're heavily invested in fantasy. No matter what's said, they usually don't listen. At the very least, it's important to note that charisma and a person's need to be rescued or saved are usually attached at the hip. Paying a little more attention to this fact should help alert people to some of the unexpected risks.

Charisma and Manipulation

As much as we've emphasized the positive aspects of charisma, it's also used by the less ethically minded for manipulation and control. Having a strong measure of social influence enables people to succeed in many areas, including venal and even criminal activities. Charisma--as a phenomenon--has no reference to the ethics of the individual blessed with its powerful properties. Expanding charisma, by developing important high-level intangibles, automatically enables individuals to achieve their goals. By the same token, there's always a risk that once these special qualities are developed they'll be used to exploit or manipulate innocent people.

As with high intelligence, there's never any assurance that charisma will be used for ethical or humanitarian purposes. We'd all hope that sophisticated problem solving skills would be used to advance the success of others--and even society--but that issue has to do with the individual's moral development or conscience. Determining whose charisma is bound by some responsible ethical code is a difficult call. Few assurances can be made that charismatic people will always operate within some ethical and responsible framework. Having said this, it's important to recognize that charisma shouldn't be blamed for bankrupt morality or criminal behavior. Only an individual's conscience can take that responsibility. It's easy and tempting to blame the wrong thing when we've been the victim of someone's manipulation.

Certain personalities--known as antisocial or sociopathic-- are conditioned into believing that they can't make progress or advance their agendas without resorting to subterfuge and manipulation. Operating on the up-and-up leaves some individuals at the mercy of their assets or deficits for securing their goals. Without deception and a host of subversive tactics, they aren't capable of making substantial progress. Although many of these people appear charismatic, it's really a superficial variety more related to sociopathy than gifted personality traits.

Charisma, unlike other calculated forms of manipulation, doesn't require deliberate deception and ethically suspect tactics.   In fact, the advantage of charisma is that manipulation and plotting aren't necessary because executing high-level intangibles enable individuals to orchestrate their agenda without resorting to unethical conduct.   That's certainly not to say that anyone who engages in strategic thinking or calculation has questionable motives.   Hardly.   Charisma simply involves expanding personal power by applying effective high-level intangibles for the betterment of others.   If a person happens to have a bankrupt sense of morality, then they might become prone toward aberrant behavior and even criminality.   It's the defect in moral development--not their refined charismatic skills--that leaves them vulnerable to exploiting others.

Learning high-level intangibles like, tact, charm, diplomacy, awareness, 'common sense,' good judgment, etc., provide an extra measure of torque to interpersonal relating.   As we've said, relating and charisma are two sides of the same coin.   Without relating effectively, charisma is just another word which carries no special impact or meaning.   With well developed relating skills, it's a powerful form of communication capable of orchestrating many difficult situations.   If communication has a powerful impact, then devious forms of manipulation aren't needed to advance one's personal agenda.   To that extent, charisma is a good safeguard against resorting to more roundabout ways of accomplishing certain goals--like lying and cheating.

When more calculated forms of manipulation are used to advance an agenda, it reflects a failure of charisma.   Unlike hard-selling or resorting to venal types of gamesmanship, charisma can't be staged or feigned. It's a spontaneous expression of verifiable personality traits which have a powerful effect on interpersonal relating. While employing strategies or tactics might represent the *politically correct* way of doing things, using charisma is just flat out *correct*. Correct in the sense that there's no deliberate setup or scheme to advance a cause or accomplish a *selfish* agenda. Manipulators don't have the personal power to influence people without constantly scheming and playing special games. While it's possible to have both charisma and manipulative tendencies, the two don't necessarily go together.

Differentiating between manipulation and charisma is sometimes difficult because it involves ferreting out certain motives which have a direct bearing on a person's intentions. Put simply, manipulators' have *selfish* motives, often exploiting others for their own gain; whereas, truly charismatic types have *altruistic* motives whose interest lies with advancing the positions and status of others. Having said this, it's still possible to have charismatic manipulators or manipulative charismatics, or, put another way, individuals who have both elements of charisma and manipulation. As we've noted, truly charismatic people display such highly refined relating and communication skills that it's not necessary to use specially designed strategies and tactics of manipulation. It's only individuals with a bankrupt sense of charisma that must revert to manipulation to accomplish their selfish agenda.

A dynamic psychotherapist, whose discoveries about human communication led to the creation of his own psychological 'church,' enlisted disenfranchised followers suffering from various forms of mental illness. Self-publishing a book on his 'revolutionary' discovery and treatment and exploiting the talk show circuit, staking claims of dramatic cures for previously hopeless patients, his organization was flooded with referrals. Processing new referrals, he would routinely place patients into intensive therapy groups designed to indoctrinate them into a paranoid state, blaming their families and friendships for their mental illness and emotional misery. Establishing his therapy center as a safe haven, he brainwashed them into believing that his therapy program was their only salvation. Once hopelessly dependent on his treatment and unable to pay, he would only retain clients who would quit-claim their real estate and donate their personal property to his center. If his patients were bereft of assets, they would quickly disappear from the program, never to be heard from again. Only those with sufficient material wealth would be retained to receive ongoing therapy. Attractive young female patients would sometimes 'trade' sexual favors for therapeutic services. At an introductory session, a prospective patient questions the 'doctor' about his program and asks:

"Dr. James, I've been suffering from chronic depression for most of my adult life. I would do anything to finally get rid of it. My psychiatrist has had me on every medication under the sun and nothing works. I have to be up-front with you--I've been suicidal in the past. I don't know how much longer I can keep struggling like this. Doctor, can you help me?"

Listening attentively and giving undivided attention, the director of the center says:

"Janice, of course I can help you. Regardless of how long you've had this terrible problem, it can be treated. You've just fallen into the wrong hands. As you already know, psychiatry doesn't have the answers. There's no 'magic bullet' with psychoactive medications. The good news is that our psychotherapeutic techniques get to the root of the problems and eliminate them for good. Our treatment completely rewires your faulty circuitry and corrects the problem. We won't drug you like your former therapist. We won't peg you--like your family has--as hopelessly depressed. And we won't blame you for being sick. We're going to begin the process of starting your life all over again."

Desperately wanting to believe the doctor's promises and experiencing some hope, Janice says:

"You're the first person who's really understood me. No one else has ever really listened to me. I've been begging my psychiatrist to get me off these damn drugs. They're just not working! Rewiring my circuitry is exactly what I need. You're the first person who's 'got it.' I can't continue living the way I feel. No one should have to live this way. Why won't anyone else listen to me? All they want to do is increase my doses of medication. I can't take it anymore--I need some help and I need it *now*."

After entering intensive group therapy, Janice is told she's headed for suicide without the therapy. The group leader informs her she must break off all relationships with the toxic influences in her life, including her mother and father and husband. She's told that her depression is directly related to her family's rejection of her and she can no longer have any further contact with them. She's invited to stay at the center until she's cured of her depression, after which she's free to leave. Believing that receiving the therapy is her last ditch attempt at survival, she's willing to pay any price and endure any hardship. She's asked to pay $100,000 for the treatment. She's shocked to learn the price of her therapy--it's her only hope of survival. She begs for a meeting with Dr. James.

At the meeting with Dr. James, she pleads with him to find some way of going through the therapy and says:

"Dr. James, I'm at the end of my rope. Without your therapy I don't know how much longer I can go on. I don't even have a fraction of the money needed to complete your treatment. Believe me, I think it's worth every penny. Please, I beg of you, find some way for me to go through your program!"

Maintaining intense eye contact and showing 'real' concern for her situation, Dr. James says:

"Janice, we're here to help people. That's why I founded the center. Many people are in exactly the same boat as yourself--unable to pay for our services. But I'm going to make another exception for you. Since you'll be living at the center, I'm going to need you to quit-claim the deed of your home to the center. Whatever your property's worth will pay for your therapy. Consider it a donation to a worthy cause: The beginning of a new life. Oh course, if this doesn't feel right to you, we'll understand. Our therapy isn't for everybody. It requires a total commitment. To start your life all over again, we have to assure that there's no turning back. You're making a *for-keeps* contract to the new you. But maybe this isn't the right time for you. Although your depression is deteriorating and you're becoming more suicidal, perhaps you're one of the people who doesn't belong here anymore. Maybe it's your time to get off the planet. We understand that and don't want to influence your decision. Remember, this is purely your choice. We know what works and what doesn't."

Trying to find her way through Dr. James' smoke, Janice seems pushed over the hump and ready to take the plunge. She remarks:

"Dr. James, please don't lose faith in me. I really want to live. What you're asking me to do is entirely reasonable. Of course I'll sign the quit-claim deed. I don't need material wealth--I need my mental health. Becoming part of your community will enable me to survive. I'm happy to sign my house over to you. By the way, I've also got a small art collection which might also help cover the costs of my therapy. You have my blessings to use whatever assets I have."

While Dr. James shows some high-level intangibles associated with charisma, his actions are far more cunning and manipulative. Making false promises regarding misleading therapeutic benefits triggers Janice's grandiose expectations that she's not a lost cause. Giving false hope-- whether it's to wannabe artists, musicians or corporate players seeking promotions--automatically creates a powerful bond leaving needy individuals vulnerable to exploitation. Even without all of Dr. James' hype and smoke, Janice's desperation for help would have generated a myriad of grandiose fantasies about his magical powers. On her own, she would have manufactured enough internal distortions to have signed away all her earthly possessions. Add to the mix, Dr. James' own manipulations and you have a lethal combination of deception paving the way to major victimization.

Recall the adage, 'when there's a need, a master will appear.' This attests to the reality that emotional and financial predators smell the blood of frail and vulnerable people. Snake oil salesmen--whether peddling magical medical treatments or sophisticated fanancial or political solutions--aren't born *only* out of their own moral defects but also their audience's demands to satisfy unmet needs. The fact that some are more charismatic than others doesn't discount that the buyer's needs contribute to this distorted perception of power and influence. As we've found in failed romantic love relationships, perceptions of the amorous parties are often so twisted that they bear little or no resemblance to reality. The young and the elderly are especially vulnerable to this kind of manipulation since their defenses against camouflaged dangers are in a more weakened state.

Certainly in Janice's case, her life-or-death struggle to survive, and her previous failures at improving her situation, left her a target of a dynamic financial predator whose criminal motives belied his specious altruistic facade. From our perspective, his behavior wasn't truly charismatic because he resorted to highly manipulative methods of influence and mind control. His intentions were clearly not in the service of someone else's success, but actually quite the opposite: Preying on and fleecing someone with legitimate needs. From the very beginning, he started making false promises about her recovery from chronic depression and suggesting that her family and friends were responsible for her problems. Then he tells her he's going to make another exception and allow her to quit-claim her real estate as her 'commitment' and payment for therapy. Next, he coerces her into believing that her condition is deteriorating and potentially fatal. Ultimately, his 'reverse psychology' manipulation, telling her, in effect, that maybe death is her preferred option, finally 'closes' her on enlisting in the program.

How many seniors are swindled out of their life-savings by con artists smelling their vulnerability? Many scams are perpetrated on the elderly precisely because of their vulnerability. It's their wishful thinking--especially about their health and financial security--that leaves them prey to predators seeking to line their pockets at the elderly's expense. Recognizing this vulnerability, the elderly should be on high alert for con artists masquerading as legitimate 'business advisors,' 'estate planners,' 'investment consultants,' or quasi-medical specialists promising cures for untreatable or chronic medical conditions over which they feel disappointed and abandoned by the limitations of conventional medicine. It's real easy to find even the most vapid and mediocre individual 'intelligent' and 'brilliant' when you're in a desperate state.

Ironically, the same vulnerability exists for the youth, whose unending search for love and identity, has them associating with some unsavory characters. Many disenfranchised youths, whose family backgrounds are missing the preferred mixture of love and stability, are drawn into subculture activities like ill-advised sex, drugs and various forms of self-mutilation like body piercing. In more extreme situations, youths actually find themselves pulled into the orbit of urban gangs and possibly enlisting in religious or secular cults. Because of abysmal neediness, charismatic leadership isn't even necessary for eventual recruitment. Although it [charismatic leadership] hastens recruitment into various groups, the process of living a chaotic existence creates--on its own--the cravings for structure sought by troubled youths.

Offered drugs, love, affection, stability and the illusion of security, many troubled youths find their way into urban gangs and various cults. Most religious leaders know that youths are easily exploited, because their unfocused and un-spent energy can be easily redirected into zealous activities. Unable to discern true charisma from dangerous manipulation, youths make easy targets for sexual and emotional predators. Although they don't usually offer predators access to instant wealth, they're conveniently exploited for labor and more perverse ambitions. Give

youth a *raison d'être*, some structure, and abundant
approval and you'll have an indefatigable following capable
of moving mountains. Converting them into various groups,
whose political and social causes bear little relevance to the
plight of youth, occurs easily. Unsuspecting youths are
especially vulnerable to the twisted motives of ambitious
manipulators.

A 17 year old female, whose parents' acrimonious divorce
caused her lingering emotional pain but whose musical,
dancing and academic talents were well rewarded with a
scholarship to a prestigious university, became involved
with a 15 year old 'born-again' adolescent. Speaking about
the bible and love of Jesus, he persuaded her to attend a
bible study given by an enthusiastic youth minister at a local
church where he worshipped. Experiencing an emotional
void in her life, she quickly bonded to the teenage boy and
his admirable adherence to scripture. Giving her a sense of
belonging and easing her emotional pain, she fell
'spiritually' in love with him. Believing that he was wise
beyond his years, she admired his devotion to Christianity.
Praising the Lord for nearly everything, he impressed her as
someone of incorruptible values and ethics. She often told
her mother about his brilliance and wisdom. When her
grades began to slip, her mother started expressing some of
her concerns:

"Bobbi, I'm really worried about you! Since getting
involved with Frankie, we've noticed your grades slipping
and you're so distant from all of us. Your own brother tells
me you've cut up his rock music CD's, telling him you're
saving him from becoming demonic. You're out with
Frankie every night of the week. It seems like you've lost
total interest in school. If you're grades slip any more,
you're risking losing your scholarship. What are you doing
every night of the week with Frankie?"

Feeling irritated with her mother's third-degree, but wanting to respond she says:

"Mother, I don't need your pressure. Frankie is the most wonderful person I've ever met. He's the only person to bring spirituality into my life. He's so wise and intelligent. Stop worrying about me. Frankie and I are spending our time at bible study discussing the scriptures. He's brought so much meaning into my life."

Not buying her story and hearing some new information about Frankie, her mother presses on with her concerns:

"One of your brother's friends tells me that Frankie dropped out of school. They tell me he's a pot-head. That doesn't sound like someone's who's got their act together. I know *you* see him as this wonderful spiritual master, but the truth is he's extremely screwed up and dragging you down with him. You're the first one in our family to ever get a scholarship to a major university. Are you going to blow it? Can't you see him for what he is . . . he's a drop out and low-life drug addict!"

Showing outward hostility toward her mother's comments, Bobbi says:

"How dare you talk about Frankie that way! He's the best thing that's ever happened to me. He brought Jesus into my life. I'll always be grateful to him. You've never liked me. You're always so critical. Don't you have anything good to say? I'm not going to listen to your s _ _ _ any more!" Breaking off her relationship with her mother, she abruptly moved out of her home and moved in with her boyfriend and his mother.

Shortly after this altercation, the mother learned that her daughter was pregnant and also using drugs under the guise of going to 'bible study.' Her daughter was forced to relinquish her scholarship and never completed college. Her mother felt devastated by her daughter's lies and tragic fall from grace. Swept away by a con artist 'talking the talk' in the born-again scene, the promising young lady was quickly derailed from the career path she had worked so hard to achieve. Because of unconscious and unresolved emotional pain from her early-life, she was easily seduced into believing her boyfriend's story. She attributed idealistic motives to his personality and couldn't see any of his obvious faults. Believing that his drug use was part of his highly evolved spirituality, she ignored all the warning signs that she was getting into bed with the wrong person. She was the last person to realize that he was exploiting her sexually, despite telling herself that their relationship was based on pure spirituality.

Situations like these are all too common when one doesn't deal with unconscious emotional factors which, if left unchecked, lead to disguised but almost guaranteed bouts of self-destructive behavior. In Bobbi's case, she was still suffering from lingering pain and anger over her parents' divorce. Blaming her mother for her parent's divorce [at least unconsciously] she decided to punish her by sabotaging her chances of fulfilling her mother's dream-- seeing her complete a college degree. Unluckily for Bobbi, she also punished herself. This is yet another example of how poor insight and awareness prevents you from developing charisma and attaining your stated goals.

What's important to remember is how unresolved emotional issues and abysmal neediness color our perceptions. In her mind, her boyfriend *was* the 'second coming' and nothing could change her beliefs. It blinded her from seeing the truth or reading the situation more objectively. As a result, she made some regrettable mistakes which cost her the better part of her future. By tuning-in to yourself, identifying your feelings, tracing them back to their roots, expressing them in a supportive atmosphere, and accepting your right to have them, otherwise self-destructive emotions can be held in check. Ignoring them opens the door to a host of unwanted complications.

While attempting to distinguish true charisma from manipulation, it's helpful to look at a person's real intentions. If the motives are venal you can rest assured that you're dealing with manipulation. If, on the other hand, you can see someone whose interest is invested in helping you succeed, then you're probably dealing with charisma. Observing excessive selfishness practically guarantees that you're encountering unacceptable levels of manipulation. Having these instincts should help you avoid becoming seduced by manipulators whose exteriors resemble people with real charisma. As for yourself, orienting your energy around advancing the causes of others, is your best assurance that you'll advance your own agenda.

Putting It All Together

I guess by now it's become clear that developing charisma is a labor-intensive process of incorporating high-level intangibles into business and everyday life. While charisma might come naturally for the lucky few, most people have to spend considerable time thinking and refining the many important qualities on which it's based. What comes instinctively to some people is alien to others. But what's important is not *how* high-level intangibles are learned but *whether* they're eventually assimilated into your style of relating. It's only by acknowledging deficiencies that individuals can identify specific areas in need of improvement. For some people, admitting faults is a sign of weakness. To those prideful people we say, 'grow up!' It's time for a change.

As we saw in Chapter 2, narcissism can be your worst enemy. It creates a false sense of pride or bravado and robs you of leaving yourself open to learning new and important skills. If you're too busy protecting your self-esteem, how can you ever admit you need help? Surely you wouldn't want people telling you you're 'great' when, in fact, you're mediocre? Or would you? Regrettably, many egocentric people crave stroking or validation at all costs and even at their own expense. It's no help if people slap you on the back when you don't deserve it. Although it feels good, it's also misleading and a poor reality- check. If you need improvement in certain areas, then for heaven's sake keep yourself open to constructive feedback.

Remind yourself continuously that you've got a lot to learn. Remember that arrogance leads to ignorance which, in turn, causes stupidity: The tendency to make the same old mistakes. We've seen this vicious cycle created by unbridled narcissism when a person's self-worth is too fragile to take in new information. You simply can't afford, in most business and social situations, to make repetitive mistakes, especially when you should have known better. There are too many situations in which one blunder, one mistake or one gaffe causes irretrievable damage. Profiting from experience and assimilating past mistakes are essential self-corrective mechanisms for attaining success in any field. As you can guess, maintaining a defensive narcissistic facade prevents this invaluable learning process from taking place.

Having said this, it's time to examine the relationship between high-level intangibles and the audience to whom these refined skills are directed. Although many people believe that competency--in whatever field--is both a game of chance *and* skill, employing high-level intangibles assures that you're expanding the skill side of the equation: You're making your own luck. Recalling the old saying, 'It's better to be lucky than good,' we've noted that it's better to be lucky *and* good. Certainly, neglecting high-level intangibles makes attaining your goals more difficult. Refining special talents helps guarantee that you'll have the skills to capitalize on the 'good' breaks once they eventually come your way.

Without having tact and savoir faire, it's difficult to negotiate your way in most business and social situations. Spending a little more time figuring out how to say something in acceptable ways, can save considerable stress and aggravation when trying to orchestrate your agenda. Tact and diplomacy require tuning-in to the impact you have on others. It's about showing basic consideration by recognizing someone else's needs. Rather than blurting things out or communicating as *you* wish, calculate your responses in ways which make others comfortable. Ignoring tact or abandoning 'common sense' makes the uphill climb of managing difficult business and social situations even steeper. Don't be ashamed to formulate your responses more carefully. It's not a form of manipulation--it's way of showing basic consideration.

While executing high-level intangibles there's often a fine line between showing charm and tact. Making deliberately obsequious remarks, with the intended effect of getting some specific result, is viewed by most people as manipulative. And yet charismatic people are frequently charming, saying and doing things which make people feel special and validated. Using charm, of course, with all its flattery and saccharine remarks, can be a form of manipulation. But, once again, it's important to recognize intentions and motives to discern whether the statements reflect true charisma or manipulation. Remember that charisma isn't a narcissistic exercise--but manipulation is invariably self-centered. People flock toward charismatic people because their lives are enhanced; while they eventually burn-out and runaway from manipulators because they wind up getting fleeced.

A CEO of a small health care corporation, whose own bravado was only exceeded by his perverted sense of humor and whose offensive behavior alienated much of his staff, prided himself on his corporate wizardry. With his starched white shirt unbuttoned to nearly his navel, his exhibitionism knew no boundaries. Addressing his staff, he would frequently make them the brunt of his sadistic jokes, often laughing hysterically after making insulting remarks. Although no one else found him funny, they felt compelled to laugh while he was cackling at his own jokes. His weekly staff meetings were dreaded because no one really knew who'd end up the target of his next joke. Blowing a lot of smoke, he claimed to be on the verge of merging his small corporation with a publicly traded health care conglomerate. Boasting how he had the 'big boys' in the palm of his hand, he was cocky about pulling off a complex merger in which he stood to make millions. At a recent acquisition meeting with the corporate players, he's found pounding his chest saying:

"Gentlemen, it's good to be here. We've got a debt free company with a 50% margin. Our revenues have escalated rapidly from $1,000,000.00 in 1994 to $6,000,000.00 in 1998, in other words more than a 6 fold increase. The present delta curve should put the company at around $10,000,000.00 per year by the year two thousand. We've established tremendous economy of scale in our management operations, streamlining staff to maximize profitability. Our clinical staff has also expanded rapidly to accommodate a dramatic increase in billable services. We're in full compliance with all government guidelines in terms of documentation and procedures. As you can see, we're a lean mean, turn-key money machine ready to be plugged into a larger corporate circuit. With your 'deep-pockets,' I intend to take this business nationwide and expand revenue 10 fold within the next year. Now, how does that sound?"

With the committee foreheads crinkled and eyebrows raised, a skeptical committee member throws him a curve ball and says:

"Mr. Blowfeld, we're also pleased to be here. We're always looking to acquire profitable corporations. It sound like you've done an amazing job sculpting this business. Clearly, it's dramatically improved from when we first met more than a year ago. Our auditors have indicated that your primary payer source, the government Health Care Financing Administration is on the verge of implementing 'managed care' which will dramatically shrink existing revenue streams, if not wipe them out entirely. We regret that our auditors have told us to pass at this time."

With his balloon rapidly leaking air, he still exhibits some bravado and tries blowing a little smoke and says:

"Of course, I think you're passing on a good deal. Actually, we're already dealing with government oversight of our program which hasn't had any effect on our revenue. Government auditors have assured me that there won't be any precipitous reductions in our program. Besides which, I've already developed a contingency plan in the event of a government shutdown of our durable income sources. As

we speak, we're already negotiating with several large
managed care companies to replace our normal funding
channels. I think you people are jumping the gun and
making a big mistake. I'm going to be in touch with your
CEO about this."

Looking a bit annoyed with his haughtiness and
unwillingness to acknowledge potential problems coming
down the pike, the committee member comments:

"You know Mr. Blowfeld . . . it's nothing personal--it's
just business. We've done our homework and made our best
call. If you really think you're going to replace your
government funding with managed care, there's a bridge in
Brooklyn we could sell you. You've got to face the music--
you're rearranging the deck chairs on the Titanic."

Before blowing too much smoke, it's advisable to do your
own homework, or, at the very least, control your narcissism
to the point that you don't think everyone else was born
yesterday. Blowfeld's pompous grandiosity, his arrogance
and defensiveness, left him incapable of dealing with
someone who couldn't be buffaloed. While his own
narcissism told him *he* could pull off any deal, his own
fantasy world prevented him from seeing reality. While *he*
knew his business was going down the tubes, he was too
arrogant to believe that someone else could reach the same
conclusion. He walked into the meeting believing that his
gift of blowing smoke could bail him out of any situation.
While he returns to his business with his tail between his
legs, he'll put a face-saving spin on the situation for his
staff.

Demonstrating arrogance or grandiosity mortally wounds
charisma by turning people off. If you're viewed as an
horse's 'rear-end,' you're not going to have any substantial

measure of long-term influence. With Blowfeld, it's only a matter of time before the smoke clears and he's alienated the better part of his sphere of influence. Unlike charismatic people, manipulators--and other sociopaths--only maintain superficial and brief relationships, until eventually having their covers blown. Once exposed, they don't last long in most settings since their presence benefits no one other than themselves. While Blowfeld clings to his small pond, it's just a matter of time until he's forced to move on to his next scam. Without touching anyone's lives in special ways, most manipulators aren't missed by too many people.

Many otherwise insoluble situations can be solved by displaying the high-level intangibles of tact and diplomacy. Tact and savoir faire enable individuals to negotiate their way through many dead-end situations. Keeping the doors of communication open is an art that requires highly evolved tact and diplomatic skills. Even where the doors seem slammed in your face, rather than expressing frustration or, worse, anger, patiently try to keep the dialogue going by developing good listening skills. Talking too much winds up getting you eventually cut off. But listening attentively-- even when you seem miles apart--continues a conversation in which the prospects of finding a workable solution are kept alive. In many respects, tact and diplomacy are about discovering special ways to make your audience feel recognized and validated.

Since we've seen what narcissism does to charisma, we've also seen the benefits of showing empathy, sensitivity and self-awareness. Taking others' needs into consideration, makes people want to go the extra mile on your behalf. Displaying conspicuous selfishness, invites unwanted impatience and intolerance. If you're trying to get ahead, it only makes sense that you'd want people to cut you more slack. Overtly insensitive acts which either offend others or contribute to perceptions of self-centeredness only contribute to your self-inflicted wounds, something most people can ill afford in business and social situations.

A likeable middle-aged homeowner, whose property was unreasonably inflated in value, is arguing to the Property Assessment Appeals Board to obtain a reduction in his assessed property value. Having done his homework, he's armed with comparable sales data indicating that the board overestimated the value of his property by $200,000.00. Approving a change in assessed value would result in a reduction in property taxes of over $2,000.00 per year or more than $166.00 per month. Since he's having trouble meeting his monthly overhead, a lot is riding on his presentation. Finally getting his chance to present his arguments, he addresses the appeals board and says:

"Forgive me for imposing on your time. I know your deputy assessors are diligent and honest workers doing their best to accurately assess property values. I also know that it's easy to either under or overestimate real estate values. With your permission, I'd like to share some normative data on comparable sales in my neighborhood. My neighborhood is especially difficult because among modestly priced homes are also homes with two and three times the value. Literally one block away from my property are homes worth triple the price. I specifically collected comps on the same block as my property. As you'll see, the comps used by your assessor were several blocks removed from my property in the high-rent district. Honest mistakes do happen and no one's to blame. With your independent review, I'm sure that you'll see the problem. Again, I want to thank all of you for your re-consideration."

Within two weeks following the meeting, the appeals board reassessed the homeowner's property and lowered the

assessed value by over $150,000.00, saving him more than
$1,500.00 per year. While he didn't get everything he asked
for, he almost did. Showing sensitivity, using respectful
language, offering face-saving statements, displaying tact,
avoiding negativity, controversy and rancor, and
incorporating diplomacy goes a long way in keeping people
open to your wishes. Just as surely, displaying arrogance,
conceit and insensitivity invites a cold shoulder and possible
retaliation. Using high-level intangibles to maintain
charisma--although difficult without practice--becomes
automatic the more you rehearse.

Timing and 'common sense' are also essential high-level
intangibles needed to orchestrate your agenda. Tact and
diplomacy are one thing, but if you're oblivious to the
circumstances and timing of events, even the gentlest and
kindest language isn't going to bail you out. As a rule of
thumb, always communicate in ways which show
consideration and respect to others' feelings--that goes
without saying. But that's not the whole story. To be
successful you must take into consideration whether
someone's even receptive to your overtures. Wanting
something doesn't necessarily mean that you're going to get
it, regardless of your strategies and tactics. It's helpful to
recognize what's appropriate in a given situation. Without
this appreciation, your best case might fall on deaf ears.
While 'common sense' doesn't come easily for many, it's
helpful to try to put yourself in someone's place, to know
what's best to do. Showing empathy is one of the best aids
in developing 'common sense.'

An elderly but practicing physician, whose wife had
recently passed away and whose family was growing
increasingly concerned about his withdrawal from social
activities, was approached--at his family's request--by a
close personal friend about introducing him to a potential

female companion. His daughter tried to talk with her father and couldn't get anywhere. Priding himself on being highly tactful and diplomatic, the doctor's older friend told the daughter that he thought he could reason with her father. Believing that it was in the father's best interest to become more socially active, he invited his physician friend to dinner to bring up the subject. At dinner, the family friend picked his best moment and posed the question:

"Jim . . . you know, I've been thinking. It's been more than three months since Sally died and you've really lost your best friend. You two were blessed with over 50 years together. No one we knew had a better marriage than you. Forgive me for sounding a bit pushy, but everyone's concerned about you. Your daughter's noticed that you don't seem to want to see the grand-kids anymore. I know it's a difficult time. But your family needs you more now than ever. This isn't the time to retreat into a shell. You've got a wonderful family who all love you very much. They want you to be part of their lives. Since Sally's gone, they've seen you become less involved. I've got a great idea. Do you remember Susie? She lost her husband almost 2 years ago and would love to get together. She's a great gal. Funny, attractive, playful--loves to go to dinner, movies, theater, sailing . . . anything you like. How about considering getting together with her? What do you say?"

Staring at his friend from across the table, Jim seemed surprised by Bill's overture and says:

"You know Bill . . . I'm just not ready to start dating anyone. It's too soon after Sally's funeral. I'm really not comfortable with that yet. Maybe sometime in the future. But now, it doesn't seem right. You might be right about the fact that I'm getting together less with my daughter, Julie, and her kids. Lately I just don't seem to have any energy. By the time I get home from the office, I'm ready for a nap. I really don't have any interest in socializing. Maybe I need to get some blood tests or something. I can't figure out what's wrong with me."

Responding to his friend's rebuff, his otherwise diplomatic friend says:

"Jim, you really need to get out and start getting back into the swing of things. Life's for the living. After all, that's what Sally would have wanted. She was a mover and shaker. She wouldn't want to see you moping around. How about it Jim? Come on--Susie's a great gal. I know you'd have a great time!"

Now feeling annoyed with his officious friend, Jim reacts:

"Bill, I've heard you. I get the picture--believe me. If I feel up to it, I'll let you know. Right now, I'm comfortable doing what I'm doing and that's it!"

The brevity and sharpness of the response indicated that Bill was getting nowhere. Although Bill exercised considerable patience and diplomacy, he was striking out. Regardless of how 'kindly' he expressed his views, the doors were slammed in his face. When the timing isn't right, no matter how well phrased your objections or arguments, you're still going to hit a brick wall. In Jim's case, only three months from his wife's departure was too soon. Had Bill or Julie approached him with the same proposition at around six months it might have been a different story.

While Bill showed passable diplomatic skills, he failed in the 'common sense' department. Recognizing that Jim's grief was usual and customary should have alerted him to the fact that Jim wasn't ready for any extra-curricular activities. Although his gesture was well-intentioned, it aggravated Jim's agitation and stress. Had Bill used more 'common sense' he might have suggested to his good buddy that he consider seeing his personal physician for a medical checkup, attending a grief group or possibly talking with a grief therapist. All of which, might have made more sense to Jim than jumping into the dating scene. Although--by anyone's standards--certainly going to dinner with Susie was hardly plunging into the singles' market.

Using timing and 'common sense' is more easily said than done because it's difficult to recognize what's appropriate in a given situation. The truth is, what works in one situation might not cut it in another. If Bill were using common sense, he wouldn't have tried so hard to sell his bereaved friend on the idea of dating. He might have explored--with comparable diplomacy and sensitivity--some of his daughter's concerns, and possibly touched on the idea of a grief group or individual therapy. As it turned out, both his timing and his 'common sense' were somewhat lacking. Retrospectively, he probably should have met with his friend without any agenda and just shown him support.

When timing and 'common sense' are in short supply, you can sometimes compensate by showing abundant energy and enthusiasm. Even with these high-level intangibles, it's no guarantee it'll get the job done. Appearing overly blasé, disinterested or lethargic can kill any deal by putting people to sleep. Saying all the right things, doesn't make up for showing low-energy. Lacking energy when relating creates instant boredom making an otherwise interesting presentation appear uncolorful and monotonous. Maintaining a high energy, on the other hand, creates excitement and is essential for advancing your agenda in most business and social situations. Perkiness or effervescence swarms people with positive energy, transforming even mediocre presentations into ones more appealing. Obviously, if you're completely bereft of substance, high energy alone won't save you. Clearly, showing abundant energy and enthusiasm awakens your audience and makes them generally more receptive.

A contractor is bidding on a multimillion dollar City Hall construction project. His bid has already won approval by the City Council, but he's still required to testify before the council for final authorization. He's told to show some enthusiasm about providing construction services to the city. During the hearing, the council president asks:

"Mr. Perez, it's good to have you here today. We've reviewed your bid and obviously like your prices and recommendations. We'd like to hear some of your views about the new City Hall renovation."

Seizing the moment and brimming with enthusiasm, the contractor says:

"It's great to be here especially under the current circumstances. I feel honored to serve this great city. Our company, as you know, has finished many challenging projects in the private sector. But getting an opportunity to change the face of our city is a great privilege. Well . . . I guess you liked my bid. I'm very excited about the City Hall renovation project. It's long overdue and our company plans to exceed all expectations outlined in the plans. We anticipate project completion at least two months before the specified deadline, and don't, at this time, expect any unforeseen costs. Refurbishing City Hall is taking our highest priority. This project will take precedent over all other company completion until we're cracking open the bottle of champagne!"

Impressed with his positive energy and enthusiasm, one of the council members asks for some clarification:

"Mr. Perez, it's good of you to join us. Welcome! On just one of your points, I was wondering if you could clarify something. When you indicate that you don't anticipate any cost overruns 'at this time,' does that mean there's a reasonable likelihood that this project will wind up going over budget?"

Remaining collected but very much wanting to respond to the council member's question, Mr. Perez remarks:

"Reviewing the budget you'll see that we've done an exhaustive cost analysis. Built into that analysis were anticipated cost increases for various building materials. Our best projections indicate that we'll actually be able to return money to the city--in other words, come in under budget. That's what we're shooting for. But, in all businesses, you can never totally rule out unexpected cost increases. And that's the closest thing I could imagine that might impact the budget on this project."

Responding to the contractor's answer, the council member remarks:

"Mr. Perez, we're very much looking forward to working with you. And I know on behalf of myself and my colleagues, we're delighted to have your company managing the City Hall remodeling project. I have no further questions."

Showing high energy and enthusiasm is contagious. Infecting his audience with the same enthusiasm, council members were impressed with Perez's presentation. It showed thoroughness, responsiveness, and, most of all, positive energy. He showed charisma by demonstrating many indispensable high-level intangibles, including, energy and enthusiasm, tact and savoir faire, 'common sense,' experience and good judgment and charm and grace under pressure. Unrattled by the council member's pointed question, he answered it enthusiastically, not showing evasiveness or annoyance. His tone was always upbeat, displaying his altruistic interest in the project, carefully disguising any selfish motives which certainly are a part of winning lucrative government contracts.

Giving reassurance is a key element to showing charisma. It's difficult to have confidence in anyone whose own needs for reassurance and validation take precedence over their interest in others. If your own maturity level demands too much self-indulgence, you're going to have a hard time convincing others to count on you. After all, how confident can you be with someone who's incapable of giving some old fashioned reassurance? Can you imagine buying anything--whether it's tangible or otherwise--without the salesperson shifting attention away from themselves and onto making you feel more comfortable? Is that really too much to ask? For some people, whose childish needs for attention and recognition consume their energy and whose inability to give to others leaves them appearing conspicuously self-centered, developing charisma is highly improbable. In order to display charisma, you must contain your narcissism and remain focused on meeting the needs of others.

Perez's high-energy focus on relieving council members' lingering concerns eventually paid off. Although they liked his bid, they loved his presentation. If he would have raised more concerns by showing defensiveness or, worse, contentiousness, they might have developed some serious reservations. As it was, he displayed the kind of charm and grace under pressure needed to allay any concerns and build confidence. By putting it all together and executing high-level intangibles, he commanded the charisma to orchestrate his agenda.

Some Final Thoughts

Like the atomic nucleus, charisma is a powerful but untapped force in human relations. While some people doubt its existence, those exposed to charismatic people are made true believers very quickly. When witnessed directly, you can't help but marvel at its power and creative potential. Although charisma's in short supply, a little bit goes a long way. Developing just a little can have a major impact on yourself and the lives of others. The fact that it can't be bottled, packaged, sold on the internet or found in a weekend growth seminar doesn't make it any less real or powerful.

As we explored the many high-level intangibles which make up charisma, we also looked at its dynamic relationship to the audience on whom we ultimately measure its effects. Trying to understand charisma without an appreciation of how it's experienced by the individuals under its spell, is like trying to analyze love outside the context of relationships. The experience of charisma is inextricably attached to the person experiencing its effects. It's even difficult to talk about charisma, without understanding its direct impact on the person who gives it its power. After all, without an audience the effects of charisma would be nonexistent.

Unmet neediness--whether it's for spiritual or romantic love, corporate advancement, family attachment, success, health or anything else--creates the dynamic of seeking out the idealized rescuer or guru. For some, the degree of charisma is directly proportionate to the intensity of their neediness. A person starved of love, for instance, whose history of failed love relationships leaves them desperate for affection and emotional security, often finds themselves idealizing their love objects in a process known as infatuation. It's usually their friends or family who keep shaking their heads and asking 'What in God's name do they see in them?'

Projecting their unmet dependency needs onto their newly found lovers, they manufacture qualities and emotions that don't really exist. In other words, their relationship is actually an artifact of an unconscious storehouse of frustrated affection. These relationships typically dissipate as quickly as they're created. Much the same way, needy individuals transfer their rescue fantasies onto people, often inflating their intentions and talents. In this way charisma is partly fabricated in proportion to a person's needs in particular areas. When abysmal neediness is mixed with dynamic personalities, the tendency toward exploitation is greatly expanded.

When confronted with charismatic people they're often swept away and become loyal followers. Fortunately for their fans, truly charismatic individuals are oriented toward improving and advancing the lives of the many people nestling under their wings. Regrettably for the needy, there are also emotional and financial predators, masquerading as well-intentioned charismatics, who are actually dangerous manipulators. They pounce on vulnerable people and exploit them for their own gains--financially, emotionally, and, yes, sexually. In extreme cases, these manipulators are found at the helm of radical groups like religious and secular cults, gangs and even some conventional political and corporate organizations.

Distinguishing charisma from manipulation is often a tough call. When someone's intentions involve exploiting others to advance their own gain, you can rest assured you're dealing with a manipulator. Although they seem charismatic, their narcissistic and self-serving propensities dominate their relationships. Charismatic people, while sometimes appearing vain and self-absorbed, are more focused on improving and advancing the lives of people with whom they're involved. Long-term relationships are rare among manipulators because it's not long before individuals grow weary of being exploited. Individuals drawn toward charismatic types, often display lasting relationships and fierce loyalty because they're consistently rewarded by remaining involved.

Examining charisma we've seen that it's based on executing many high-level intangibles, including (a) savor faire, tact and face-saving, (b) 'common sense,' (c) diplomacy, (d) timing, (e) awareness and insight, (f) politeness and manners, (g) energy and motivation, (h) experience and good judgment, (I) drive and desire, (j) charm, class and grace under pressure and (k) playfulness and humor. Paying closer attention to your own internal dynamics, namely your emotions and beliefs, and rehearsing these helpful elements, will enable you to expand your level of charisma. Although you may be your own worst critic and incapable of seeing your progress, acquiring a little charisma goes a long way in most situations. How much you need to advance your agenda is anyone's guess, but adding charisma to your existing skills puts the extra octane in your tank for achieving your goals.

Points to Remember

- Acknowledge that charisma does, in fact, exist

- Accept that learning charisma might come easier to some than others

- Realize that charisma can, in fact, be learned

- Rehearse high-level intangibles whenever possible

- Control narcissistic propensities

- Orient yourself around meeting the needs of others

- Recognize the difference between charisma and manipulation

- Accept that ethical or moral defects have nothing to do with charisma

- Admit that excessive neediness causes vulnerability to manipulation

- Identify and deal with unconscious emotions and beliefs impacting charisma

- Maintain openness to constructive feedback

- Give abundant reassurance, support and validation to others

Some Concluding Thoughts

Like panning for gold, it's taken considerable effort and, yes, perseverance, to eventually get to the bullion. Finding the nuggets of charisma has led us down the path of exploring *high-level intangibles*, those special qualities which, when properly executed, generate charisma. While it's probably true that it comes more naturally to some, it's also true that charisma can, in fact, be learned. As with all types of learning, remain open to feedback. And as you begin to make progress, control your self-criticism and reward your progress lavishly.

Paying closer attention and executing important high-level intangibles noticeably expands a person's charisma. But, having said this, that's clearly not the whole story. We also know that remaining narcissistic or consumed with your own needs, writes a toxic prescription negating charisma and personal power. Regardless of how hard you try to develop these high-level intangibles, if you're excessively self-centered, they won't work. Manipulation--or using people for your own gain--only lasts so long before you turn people off and lose your personal power.

Charisma is driven by the need to improve and advance the lives of others. Greed and self-consumption short-circuit its powerful effects. Selfishness, unsightly vanity and exploitive intentions drain charisma like an old battery. The power--and magic--of charisma is derived from the desire to expand the lives of others. *Giving*--not taking--generates its energy. By giving generously, charisma creates its irresistible affinity, leading to satisfying relationships and eventual popularity. Charismatic people are placed on a pedestal not because they're better at executing spin or blowing smoke but precisely because they deliver abundant rewards to the people with whom they're involved.

The notion that 'private interest is best served by public interest' attests to the fact that reaping society's biggest rewards are reserved for those who also put out the most effort on behalf of people. You see, it's really OK to be selfish as long as you're also satisfying the needs of others. By meeting your own needs and committing yourself to multiplying the success of others, you'll assure that charisma is an essential part of *your* personality.